The Rock and Roll Movie Encyclopedia of the 1950s

To my brother, Steve
who brought rock and roll into the house...
and Kevin Fernan
who continues to bring rock and roll into the house

The Rock and Roll
Movie Encyclopedia
of the 1950s

MARK THOMAS McGEE

McFarland & Company, Inc., Publishers
Jefferson, North Carolina, and London

The Author

British Library Cataloguing-in-Publication data are available

Library of Congress Cataloguing-in-Publication Data

McGee, Mark Thomas, 1947–
 The rock and roll movie encyclopedia of the 1950s / by Mark Thomas
McGee.
  p.   cm.
 [Includes index.]
 Includes bibliographical references.
 ISBN 0-89950-500-7 (lib. bdg. : 50# alk. paper)
 1. Rock films—History and criticism.   I. Title.
PN1995.9.M86M4   1990
791.43′657—dc20   89-43657
                                                                              CIP

Manufactured in the United States of America

McFarland & Company, Inc., Publishers
 Box 611, Jefferson, North Carolina 28640

Contents

Foreword

Back in the 1930s, Benny Goodman got so fed up with the bland music he and his band were expected to play that he threw all caution to the wind one evening at the Palomar Ballroom in Hollywood and told his boys to bust loose. It was toward the end of the evening and everyone in the joint had been lulled into a zombie-like trance. Goodman managed to snap them out of it, and the King of Swing was born. Sadly, two decades later, popular music had reverted to the anesthetic state that Goodman had found so appalling.

Into this swamp of boredom came rock and roll, a hybrid of country swing and rhythm and blues, and what a stink it caused. Frank Sinatra called it "the most brutal, ugly, vicious form of expression" he'd ever heard—sly, lewd and dirty. Jimmy Snow, the pastor of a Southern Baptist church, told his congregation that the music was dangerous. How did he know? Because of the way it made him feel... the fire down below. Award-winning composer Dimitri Tiomkin thought the music indicated that the country was reverting to "savagery," and the most obvious indication of it was the number of concerts that had erupted in violence. "[The teenagers] will tell you they get a 'charge' out of rock 'n' roll," said Tiomkin. "So do the kids who smoke marijuana and shoot 'H'." But when Benny Goodman was asked what he thought about rock music, he replied: "I guess it's OK man, at least it has a beat."

Apparently Goodman was the only one who remembered his history, for a prominent New York psychiatrist had once warned the readers of *The New York Times* about the "dangerously hypnotic influence of swing." During the Jazz Age an upstate New York preacher chastised the music for its "lawlessness, lasciviousness, and savage animalism." And Ol' Blue Eyes must have forgotten about the afternoon

10,000 of his fans tore the boxoffice apart at the Paramount Theater in New York where he was performing. Traffic was blocked, bystanders trampled, and store windows broken. It took 700 riot police and 200 patrolmen to restore order. Yet when *Rock Around the Clock* (the first motion picture about rock and roll music) was banned in some parts of England and America because there were some people who didn't know how to behave themselves, it was as if it was all happening for the first time. Sam Katzman, the producer of *Rock Around the Clock,* had a simple rebuff: *Don't Knock the Rock!*

The first rock movie I saw was *Loving You* with Elvis Presley. I was ten years old and I thought the movie was wonderful. During the "Mean Woman Blues" number I started clapping my hands to the beat. Soon everyone in my row was doing the same. Before long the whole theatre (or so it seemed) had joined in. It was wonderful! Then the lights came on and the movie stopped and an anonymous voice over the P.A. system warned that the theatre would be cleared if there were any further demonstrations. I couldn't understand why they'd done it. I didn't know they were afraid we'd tear the place apart. I hadn't heard about all of the trouble attributed to R&R music. I didn't know about the sailor who was repeatedly stabbed by a gang of teen-aged punks just outside of the arena in Boston where Alan Freed was having one of his shows.

In San Jose, at a Fats Domino concert, some bozo threw a beer bottle at a group of dancers and what followed was described by the city's police chief as "the wildest riot in the history of our city." The incident nearly caused a ban on rock and roll shows in California.

When Columbia Pictures released *Rock Around the Clock* in 1956, many exhibitors were afraid of similar riots in their theatres. Projectionists were often instructed to keep the volume low and the house lights up.

"I personally felt that the kids never took those pictures seriously," said John Ashley, the star of many youth-oriented movies. The actor felt it was ridiculous that people made such a fuss about the films. How could they be blamed for inciting delinquent behavior when the kids were laughing at them? Dorothy Shensa Miller, in an article written for *Boxoffice* (an exhibitor magazine), agreed:

> First of all, generally speaking, no manager blames the type of picture shown for the delinquent behavior of a juvenile. It's true of course, that certain films excite and arouse the viewers, and may contribute to some extent to the sort of behavior which might be the result of "high emotions." . . . However, assuming that such is the case, the particular type

of juvenile audience which starts trouble because he is affected by what he has seen on the screen would be just as likely to react to any of hundreds of other circumstances—via subtle ad suggestions, television, books, etc.

Still, worried exhibitors wanted some assurance their theatres would survive a rock and roll program. To that end, the following rules were enforced in many theatres across the country:

1. Juvenile theatregoers must be made to recognize authority—whether in the garb of a policeman or the manager himself. No disturbance should be overlooked. For the slightest suggestion of a misdemeanor, the guilty party should be asked to leave and, if necessary, forced to do so. In this way, the theatre will get a reputation for being "strict," and young people, inclined to be trouble-makers, will not attempt this more than once.

2. A set standard for dress should be adhered to. If boys are made to wear jackets to be admitted—even if they remove them once they are seated—and if admittance is denied to dungaree-wearing girls or boys—the general "tone" of the house will be uplifted.

3. A set of rules stating company policy as to dress, roaming around, disturbing others, etc. (such as "no smoking" signs), should be prominently displayed in the rest rooms and at various places in the theatre—and should be strictly adhered to.

4. No manager should be afraid to deny admittance to anyone if they seem to be undesirable—whether their appearance is so unkempt as to suggest a reflection of their behavior, or whether they are boisterous, or if they come as a gang—using the term restrictively to connote the meaning of organized delinquents. Law enforcement agencies will, if called upon, back up any manager denying anyone admission.

5. Generally, it is agreed that girls are by far the worst offenders and usually are at the root of most of the trouble. To offset this, the manager and ushers should constantly patrol the aisles and see that proper behavior is kept.

6. Because they are more familiar with their own audience and what might be good or bad boxoffice—not only as far as receipts are concerned—managers feel that they should have more of a "voice" in selection of features to be exhibited.

It's my feeling that most rock and roll movies, especially the ones covered by this book, were more likely to incite unseemly behavior because of their banality more than anything else. Snip the musical interludes from most rock and roll movies of the period and what's left is an endurance test that would push anyone's patience to the breaking point. Why then should anyone want to read a book about them, much less write one? The answer is simple: These early rock movies provide what is often the only visual record we have of the rock and roll legends in their prime. These movies were the rock videos of their day, and the purpose of this volume is to provide a background of not only the films but the performers in them. A number of authors have attempted this task, but their information seems to be based either on old memories or on studio press material, which is often incorrect. For this book I have made every effort to go right to the source, regardless of how painful some of these films might have been to sit through.

However, try as I did, some of these films simply could not be had, and the reader should be cautioned that portions of the text may be incorrect.

Some of the films listed in this volume, like *High School Confidential,* aren't rock and roll movies per se, but they do contain rock performances. So you'll find movies like *Blood of Dracula* and *The Giant Gila Monster* listed. Missing are films like *Running Wild* and *Beginning of the End,* which had rock music played on a jukebox or radio. Performers of the music must be onscreen for the film to rate an entry. And movies like *Gidget* and *Bernadine* are absent because, in spite of their inclusion in most rock movie books, there is no rock music in them. (In this regard I did bend the rules a bit for *Love Me Tender,* since the songs in that film are not rock songs. They are, however, performed onscreen by the King of Rock and Roll, and no doubt would have been rock songs had the film's period allowed . . . therefore this exception.)

I want to thank all of the people who helped me with this endeavor. Let's start with Randy Robertson, who actually had the idea to do this book in the first place and the good sense not to. Bob Villard and Alan Lungstrum supplied the bulk of the visual material. Then there were the people who were kind enough to share memories: John Ashley, Roger Corman, Alex Gordon, Charles Griffith, Dick Miller, Lori Nelson, Max Rosenberg, John Saxon, Russ Tamblyn, and Mamie Van Doren. And thanks to all the people whose album notes supplied me with information I needed: John Beecher, Roy Carr, Jonathan Green, Tim Hauser, Gary Herman, Philip Jenkinson, Malcolm Jones, Paul Lichter, Lynn Ellis McCutchen, Guy Remark, Greg Shaw, Bruce Solomon, Michael Uslan and Alan Warner. Thanks also to Chuck Cirino, Don Glut, Marty Kearns, and Fred Olen Ray. And thanks to you for reading this book.

Mark McGee
Arcadia, California

Rock Around the Clock

THE FILMS

Because They're Young (1960)

Adapted from John Farris' novel *Harrison High* and released during the middle of the payola scandal, *Because* more or less marked the end of the rock and roll movie. The choice of Dick Clark in the leading role couldn't have been more appropriate.

Clark was the host of TV's "American Bandstand" on ABC five days a week, hitting an estimated 40,000,000 homes. Clark seemed to be one of the kids even though he was thirty and wore a suit. Anyone who ever watched the show will know what you mean when you say, "I'll give it a nine because it has a beat and you can dance to it." Clark had the kids on his show rate the new platters he played and dance to the big hits. Some of the regular dancers on his show became minor celebrities. But if you can set nostalgia aside, "American Bandstand" was pretty limp stuff. The singers Clark favored were better at ballads than rock and were mostly white. Clark was, in a sense, the anti–Alan Freed. And he was a whole lot shrewder. During the payola scandal Clark came out smelling like a rose. Freed was slapped with a fine, given a six-month suspended sentence, and still had a grand jury on his ass for income tax evasion when he died in 1965.

There was a song at the time called "The Old Payola Roll Blues," but it's doubtful that Dick Clark ever played it on his show. It referred to the disc jockeys being summoned to answer charges that they took bribes to play music. It was true, of course, but you could bet even money the men accusing them were doing the same in their fashion. There was already an investigation into quiz-show rigging going on. Senator Owen Harris and his Senate subcommittee had nabbed Charles Van Doren, an English instructor at Columbia University, who developed an incredible following during his winning streak on the TV quiz show "Twenty-One." Over 25 million viewers sweated with him through week after week of incredibly difficult questions until one of his

3

Ad for *Because They're Young.*

defeated opponents blew the whistle. Herbert Stempel told the New York District Attorney's office the show was a phoney. Van Doren was called before Harris' subcommittee and after a year of denial finally confessed he'd been given the answers in advance. Van Doren told the committee he didn't think at the time that it was that big a deal. After all, it wasn't much different from wrestling. It was show business. Besides, it had a good effect on the national attitude toward teachers, education and intellectual life. And he was also winning more money than he'd ever dreamed of.

Senator Harris was on a roll, and it didn't take the folks at ASCAP long to convince him he could stay on a winning streak by turning his attention to rock and roll disc jockeys. Plenty of people hated rock music. The DJs were easy targets. The only people Harris would piss off by his investigation, besides the DJs of course, were the kids, and they didn't vote so what did it matter? The reason ASCAP (American Society of Composers, Authors and Publishers) instigated this attack was that they'd lost control of rock and roll. Once ASCAP made money on sheet music, piano rolls, and recordings. But when radio came into its own, stations battled with ASCAP over royalty payments, and some stations refused to play anything registered with ASCAP. The Broadcast Music Incorporated (BMI) was formed to pick up the slack, and BMI ended up with most of the rock songs because ASCAP didn't want to soil its hands with black music and hillbilly music. When rock and roll turned the music business upside down, ASCAP found themselves on the outside looking in. So they convinced Senator Harris to gun down the competition legally. It would, after all, be mutually beneficial to them both. Besides, that God-awful rock music had gotten too darned big for its britches.

With zest and vigor, the subcommittee went after those disc jockeys the way Senator McCarthy had chased after those communists, and who was to say there was much difference between the two? For all anyone knew, rock and roll *was* a communist plot to undermine the moral fiber of our children.

Alan Freed refused to testify.

Dick Clark, who owned a piece of Jamie Records and other little companies and their songs, said his investments were for tax purposes. But if the government didn't think it was right then neither did he. He got rid of everything but his interests in "American Bandstand." The committee left Clark alone and went after Freed, who found himself in a bigger game than he'd expected. The committee made sure Freed was fired and that he'd have a lot of trouble finding work again. He was poison. Rock and roll was poison. Frightened disc jockeys refused to play rock, understandably, and popular music reverted to the sound it had had just prior to rock. It had a slightly livelier bounce, but Bobby Rydell, who sings the most energetic song in *Because They're Young*, isn't so very far away from Dean Martin. In 1959 the top-selling song in

Because They're Young. Top: Warren Berlinger (left) and Roberta Shore are two of the students helped by devoted teacher Dick Clark (right). Bottom: Duane Eddy and the Rebels cue up to play "Shazam."

the nation was "Mack the Knife" by Bobby Darin, a song that could just as easily have been a hit for Frank Sinatra.

A few years ago, around 1985, an investigation into MCA's financial records began, instigated by the United States Department of Justice. They discovered that payments had been made to Salvatore Pisello, who had ties with the mob. And the more Federal agents looked, the more corruption they found, on all fronts. Money had changed hands without the government getting its share, and if that isn't worse than burning the flag, I don't know what is. And there's a smell of payola everywhere you turn these days.

In *Because They're Young* Dick Clark is cast as a devoted, tireless high school teacher. Clark held a contest on his Saturday night show for a month to see who'd get to see his movie for free, a movie which was partly owned by Clark's Drexel productions. Say, doesn't that sound like...?

The Music

Duane Eddy, the twangy guitar player from New York, spent most of his youth in Arizona, listening to old Chet Atkins records. A demo of "Rebel Rouser" got him a contract with Dick Clark's Jamie Records. The song was a big hit as was Eddy's version of "Because They're Young" which is sung in the film by James Darren. But it was Eddy's version, orchestrated by Don Costa, that became a hit. The song on the flipside is the one Eddy performs in the film.

Bobby Rydell, whose hair was almost as high as Little Richard's, flourished during the payola period of music. He popped up on TV now and then in dramatic roles, and he continued to produce hit after hit—"Wild One," "Volare," "Swingin' School"—the latter sung in *Because They're Young.* His appearance in Columbia's wheezing *Bye, Bye Birdie* was eclipsed by the new sound from England, led by a group called The Beatles, who remembered what rock and roll sounded like. Good thing, too, since everyone in the United States had forgotten.

James Darren: "Because They're Young," available on Colpix (which, like Jamie Records, were good for about one play. After that the records sounded like you'd played 'em a billion times).

Duane Eddy: "Shazam," available on Jamie.

Bobby Rydell: "Swingin' School," available on Capitol.

The Reception

"The oldsters may want to stay home and watch TV.... In his movie debut, Dick Clark's his familiar, likable self."—*Photoplay*.

"The popularity of Dick Clark with the younger set no doubt will exert a strong boxoffice appeal."—*Film Daily*.

"The appeal that has made [Dick Clark] a TV fave and spokesman for this particular bracket brightens an interesting and refreshing feature as Clark scores heavily."—*Variety*.

"While it is aimed at younger audiences, it is also a considerably better than routine exploitation film."—*Motion Picture Herald*.

"Try not to miss it."—*Screen World & TV*.

The Cast

Dick Clark (Neil), Michael Callan (Griff), Tuesday Weld (Anne), Victoria Shaw (Joan), Roberta Shore (Ricky), Warren Berlinger (Buddy), Doug McClure (Jim), Linda Watkins (Frances McCalla), Chris Robinson (Patcher), Rudy Bond (Chris), Wendell Holmes (Mr. Donlan), Philip Coolidge (Mr. Rimer), Bart Patton (Kramer), Stephen Talbot (Eric), Kathryn Card (Mrs. Wellenberg), Paul Genge (Pekarek), Susan Odin (plump girl), Frances Karath (girl friend).

The Credits

Director Paul Wendkos, *Producer* Jerry Bresler, *Screenplay* James Gunn from the novel *Harrison High* by John Farris, *Director of Photography* Wilfrid Cline, A.S.C., *Art Director* Robert Peterson, *Editor* Chester W. Schaeffer, *Sound* Josh Westmoreland, *Assistant Director* Jerrold Bernstein, *Music* Johnny Williams. B&W 102 min. Drexel Pictures Corporation Production. A Columbia Picture.

The Big Beat (1958)

Like all of the rock films from Universal-International, *The Big Beat* attempted to appeal to a broader market by eliminating the delinquency angle often associated with rock films and in this instance by mixing other forms of music—calypso, jazz, pop, etc.—into the brew. The film also was a sort of screen test for pop singer Gogi Grant, who no doubt hoped it would lead to a career in films.

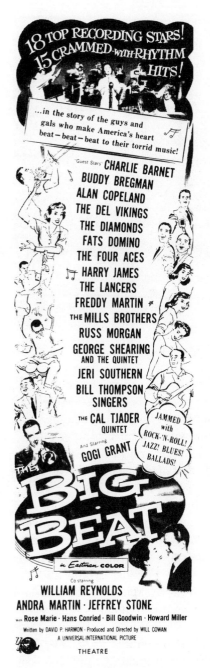

Ad for *The Big Beat.*

Gogi Grant (whose real name is Audrey Arinsberg) had a monster hit record in 1956, "The Wayward Wind," originally written for a man by Herb Newman and Stan Lebousky. A few of the lyrics were changed so that it could be sung from a woman's point of view, and it was released on Newman's Era records.

The eldest of six children, Gogi Grant was born in Philadelphia in 1924 or 1936. When she was twelve her family moved to Los Angeles. She started thinking about becoming a singer when she was in high school. She entered a talent contest, met a vocal coach and made a demo record, but an MCA talent scout said she wasn't ready. A few days after the scout made this pronouncement, the head of the music department at MCA returned from vacation and played the demo, which had been left on his turntable. The department head got her an audition and a contract with RCA, but her records there didn't click. It wasn't until she signed with Era and recorded "Suddenly There's a Valley" that her career was launched. Despite her top billing in *The Big Beat*, her role is secondary to William Reynolds and Andra Martin, a couple of U-I's young contract players (later reunited for the studio's *The*

The Four Aces croon to the crowd in *The Big Beat*.

Thing That Couldn't Die). Reynolds played the son of a successful record company executive who had a devil of a time convincing his old man to add a little rock and roll to the company's roster. Conveniently, this simple story didn't interfere very often with the musical interludes.

Among the rock and roll artists who perform in the film are The Diamonds, a white group from Canada that made a career out of covering songs by black groups. Dave Somerville, Bill Red, Ted Kowalski, and Phil Leavitt were on their way to their first gig (in the basement of a church) when Kowalski thought of the name for the group. They were discovered by disc jockey Bill Randle, who took them to Mercury records in Chicago. There they cut their first record, "Why Do Fools Fall in Love?" which had been a hit for Frankie Lymon and the Teenagers. "Little Darlin'," a song written by Maurice Williams and originally recorded by the Gladiolas, was the Diamonds' biggest hit, which they sing in *The Big Beat*.

The Del Vikings, reportedly the first integrated group, sing one number in the film. Norman Wright, Corinthian "Kripp" Johnson, Donald "Gus" Bakus, David Lerchey, and Clarence E. Quick met and began singing together while they were in the military. Wright was from Pennsylvania, Johnson from Maryland, Bakus and Quick from New York and Lerchey from Indiana. In 1957 the group had its first hit record, "Come Go with Me," written in five minutes by Clarence Quick and recorded in a Pittsburgh disc jockey's basement. It was originally sold to the small Fee Bee records, later picked up by Dot, who quickly signed the group to a contract. But with the exception of Johnson, they were all under age at the time, so when Mercury records offered a sweeter deal everyone but Johnson left and William Blakely was hired to take his place. Johnson formed another group, all black, and recorded "Whispering Bells" for Dot while the other Del Vikings went to work on "Cool Shake" over at Mercury. By the end of the year Mercury got control of the group's name, but no hits followed. The only member of the original group still active is Quick.

There are more non-rockers than anything else in *The Big Beat*, and probably the hottest of the bunch were The Four Aces with Al Alberts, Dave Mahoney, Sod Vaccaro and Lou Silvestri, a group that hailed from Philadelphia. Their biggest hit was "Love Is a Many Splendored Thing," which had been turned down by Tony Martin, Nat Cole, Doris Day, and Eddie Fisher—all of whom rushed to record it when it went to the top of the charts in 1955. The Four Aces were already familiar to U-I, having recorded the title song to one of the studio's biggest films of 1956, *Written on the Wind*. In *The Big Beat* they sing one of their typical ballads, yet the same year the film was released they recorded something called "Rock and Roll Rhapsody," which might have been more appropriate.

The radio spot says it all: "The happiest combination ever is coming your way. Two wonderful motion pictures filled to the brim with music, laughter, dancing, young love for all the family. *Summer Love* and *The Big Beat* . . . *Summer Love*, the wonderful successor to *Rock Pretty Baby* and its teenage music makers . . . *The Big Beat* with 18 top recording guest stars! Fifteen sweet 'n' solid songs from jazz to swing to rock 'n' roll! Be happy, stay happy with *Summer Love* and *The Big Beat!*"

The Music

Alan Copeland and Russ Morgan Orchestra: "As I Love You."
The Del Vikings: "Can't Wait."
Fats Domino: "The Big Beat" and "I'm Walking," available on Imperial.

The Diamonds: "Little Darlin'" and "Where Mary Go," available on Mercury.

The Four Aces: "Take My Heart," released on Decca.

Gogi Grant: "Call Me," "Lazy Love" (with Harry James), and "You've Never Been in Love," released on an RCA Victor EP with the song "I Waited So Long" which is performed in the film by Jeri Southern and the Cal Tjader Quintet.

The Mills Brothers: "You're Being Followed," released on Decca.

Rose Marie, The Lancers and The Paulette Sisters: "It's Great When You're Doing a Show."

The George Shearing Quintet: "As I Love You."

Jeri Southern: "I Waited So Long."

Cal Tjader Quintet: "I Waited So Long."

The Reception

". . . has plenty for the exhibitor to sell to young audiences, but it somehow should be got across to mature customers that this is not one of those rackety rock and roll offerings that drum mother and dad out of the theater." — *Variety.*

"This picture seemed to please. Did as well as a good western for the Friday-Saturday change." — Mel Danner, an exhibitor in Oklahoma.

"It had too much slow music but my rock 'n' roll fans liked it otherwise." — Victor Weber, an exhibitor in Arkansas.

"As musicals go it is fair, but was very disappointing to the younger set, as they were expecting rock 'n' roll and did not get it." — Harold Bell, an exhibitor in Quebec.

"While [it] doesn't have a strong beat, it is a mildly pleasant one. . . . Irving Glassberg's camera action manages to give freshness to conventionally static sequences. . . ." — *The Hollywood Reporter.*

"Took a tip from a very nice *Exhibitor Has His Say* report and played this on Sunday-Monday, following a Thursday-Friday-Saturday run of *Country Music Holiday. Country Music* seemed to get the folks in the mood for *The Big Beat* because they came and saw and liked and told us so. More young folks out to the Sunday-Monday change than we've had for quite a while." — Carl Veseth, an exhibitor in Montana.

The Cast

Charlie Barnet (himself), Buddy Bregman (himself), Alan Copeland (himself), The Del Vikings (themselves), The Diamonds (themselves), Fats Domino (himself), The Four Aces (themselves), Harry James (himself), The Lancers (themselves), Freddy Martin (himself), The Mills Brothers (themselves), Russ Morgan (himself), George Shearing and the quintet (themselves), Jeri Southern (herself), The Bill Thompson Singers (themselves), The Cal Tjader Quintet (themselves), Gogi Grant (Cindy Adams), William Reynolds (Johnny Randall), Andra Martin (Nikki Collins), Jeffrey Stone (Danny Phillips), Rose Marie (Ma Gordon), Hans Conried (Vladimir), Bill Goodwin (Joseph Randall), Howard Miller (himself), Jack Straw, Phil Harvey, Ingrid Goude, Steve Drexel.

The Credits

Producer-Director Will Cowan, *Screenplay* David P. Harmon, *Director of Photography* Irving Glassberg, *Art Director* Alexander Golitzen and Eric Orborn, *Sound* Leslie I. Carey and Corson Jowett, *Editor* Edward Curtiss, *Music* Henry Mancini. Color 82 min. Universal-International.

Sources

Boxoffice Vol. 73, No. 4, May 19, 1958, pg. 116; Vol. 73, No. 22, September 22, 1958, pg. 4; Vol. 74, No. 4, November 17, 1958, pg. 10; Bronson, *Billboard Book of Number One Hits;* Nite, *Rock On;* Stambler, *Encyclopedia of Pop Rock and Soul.*

Blood of Dracula (1957)

This film mixed elements from old vampire movies and juvenile delinquency melodramas and wrapped the whole business in a mad scientist motif. As many horror films of the period were aimed at the youth market (as this one was), songs were often inserted into the proceedings to further establish a rapport with young audiences. As often as not, however, in addition to being lame, the songs weren't rock and roll and tended to alienate rather than woo. One explanation for this could be that the people making the horror and science fiction films of the fifties

Jerry Blaine gets an undeserved reward from two enthusiastic young ladies after singing his own composition, "Puppy Love," in *Blood of Dracula*.

were well past teenage themselves and most likely didn't understand or enjoy rock music. Although his *Beginning of the End* contained a rock song ("Natural, Natural Baby") during its pre-credit sequence, producer-director Bert I. Gordon chose a nondescript ballad for his *Attack of the Puppet People* the following year, "You're a Dolly," sung by Marlene Willis. Gordon was 36 when he made the film. The producer of *Blood of Dracula*, Herman Cohen, was 30 when he commissioned Jerry Blaine to write "Eeny Meeny, Miney Mo," a forties-style song, for his *I Was a Teenage Werewolf* in 1957. Blaine is closer to rock with the song he wrote for Cohen's *Blood of Dracula*, a somber piece called "Puppy Love." It may be significant to note that just after Kenny Miller sings Blaine's song in *Teenage Werewolf* he is punched in the nose, and in *Blood of Dracula* Blaine's number so irritates a frustrated teacher that she transforms one of her students into a murderous vampire.

The story by Herman Cohen and Aben Kandel is a variation on

their previous werewolf movie with the principal characters switched from male to female. A troubled teen, played by Sandra Harrison, is dumped into Sherwood's School for Girls after her father remarries. Miss Harrison, as Nancy, is turned into a vampire through hypnosis and the power of an ancient Carpathian amulet by her frigid science teacher, Miss Branding, who thinks the governments of the world will stop making bombs when they realize people can be turned into vampires. When Nancy realizes what's happening she kills the old bag but dies during the struggle.

During all of this there's time for Jerry Blaine to sing his song. Blaine hailed from Texas, born in 1936. He was two when his family moved to California, and for a while he toured with the King Brothers Circus as an acrobat before going to New York to study acting.

The film's director, Herbert L. Strock, said he read a review of the movie that called it the worst vampire picture ever made. It's far from that but even further away from the best.

The Music

Jerry Blaine: "Puppy Love."

The Reception

". . . part of an American-International package with *I Was a Teenage Frankenstein* . . . a surefire exploitation package." — *The Hollywood Reporter*.

"Slow in takeoff, film nevertheless packs enough interest to hold its audience. . . . Jerry Blaine, one of the victims, is in for a tuneful song number . . . handled effectively. . . ." — *Variety*.

". . . the type of entertainment that should get over in the action houses, especially for audiences who like the shockers." — *Film Daily*.

The Cast

Sandra Harrison (Nancy Perkins), Louise Lewis (Mrs. Branding), Gail Ganley (Myra), Jerry Blaine (Tab), Heather Ames (Nola), Malcolm Atterbury (Lt. Dunlap), Don Devlin (Eddie), Tom Brown Henry (Mr. Perkins), Jeanne Dean (Mrs. Perkins), Richard Devon (Sgt. Stewart), Paul Maxwell (Mike), Shirley DeLancey (Terry), Michael Hall (Glenn).

The Credits

Director Herbert L. Strock, *Producer* Herman Cohen, *Screenplay* Ralph Thornton, *Director of Photography* Monroe Askins, *Art Director* Leslie Thomas, *Editor* Robert Moore, *Sound* Herman Lewis, *Music* Paul Dunlap.

Bop Girl Goes Calypso (1957)

Bop Girl went before the cameras on March 19, 1957, and by the time it was ready for release, its leading lady, Judy Tyler, had completed her role in *Jailhouse Rock* and had been killed in an auto accident.

The movie was made by the team of Aubrey Schenck and Howard W. Koch. In 1955 and 1956 these two made seventeen pictures under their Bel-Air banner — *Shield for Murder, Yellow Tomahawk, Three Bad Sisters, Pharaoh's Curse,* and others.

Schenck began his association with UA as a legal consultant one year after getting his degree in law at New York University in 1933. Later he was engaged by National Theatres Amusement Company as an attorney and film buyer, a position he held from 1935 until 1941, when he went to work for 20th Century–Fox's Spyros Skouras as an executive assistant. *Shock* was Schenck's first film as a producer. Later, at Eagle-Lion, he continued to produce economically made action pictures. When Eagle-Lion folded Schenck moved to Universal-International and decided to go into independent production.

Singer Harry Belafonte opened the door to calypso music in the mid-fifties with his enormously popular song "Banana Boat (Day-O)." In *Bop Girl,* Bobby Troup (a singer-writer himself) plays a university psychologist who tries to prove that calypso music will eventually replace rock and roll. (Of course, if he simply waited he'd find out if he was right or wrong without a lick of research.) Troup convinces a lady rocker to give the new music a try. She mixes calypso and rock and roll and comes up with a new sound that sweeps the nation.

The job of creating this "new" sound was given to Les Baxter. Originally a musical arranger for Capitol, Baxter had a couple of instrumental hit records before getting into film scores. He scored a dozen or more Bel-Air films and later went to work for American-International, where he scored practically everything that came out of the company after 1960. Baxter wrote six of the fourteen tunes for *Bop Girl.*

Ad for *Bop Girl Goes Calypso.*

The Music

The information that follows is based solely on the pressbook, which lists the groups and the songs but not who does what. As the movie was unavailable for screening there is really no way to know if all of these songs were actually in the film or if all of the titles are correct. And with no further information (apparently little has been written about it), the film appears in this volume primarily to keep the title alive.

The performers: The Mary Kaye Trio, The Goofers, Lord Flea, Nino Timpo, The Titans, and The Cubanos.

The songs or instrumentals: "Rovin' Gal," "Calypso Boogie," "Way Back in San Francisco," "De Rain," "Oo Ba Lo," "Hard Rock and Candy Baby" (all written by Les Baxter with either Jim Baxter or Lenny Adelson), "Calypso Rock" (sung by the Mary Kaye Trio), "Fools Rush In," "I'm Gonna Rock and Roll Till I Die" (the Goofers), "Wow," "Calypso Jamboree" (Lord Flea), "Rhythm in Blues," "So Hard to Laugh, So Easy to Cry," and "Horn Rock" (Nino Tempo).

The Reception

"For the fan of popular music, the picture will be a feast, and as such its exploitation possibilities are strong. In terms of story, however, the picture treads routine ground." — *Film Daily.*

The Goofers perform "I'm Gonna Rock and Roll Till I Die" in *Bop Girl Goes Calypso*, shortened to *Bop Girl* when the calypso craze had run its course.

"It must have been the few rock and roll pieces that held it up." — Harold Bell, a Quebec exhibitor.

". . . Aubrey Schenck . . . and Howard W. Koch . . . never give the impression that they are slumming when they do a picture that is frankly designed to make money. The presentation has pace, variety and a pleasant cast. . . ." — *The Hollywood Reporter*.

The Cast

Judy Tyler (Jo Thomas), Bobby Troup (Robert Hilton), Margo Woode (Marion Henricks), Lucien Littlefield (Professor Winthtrop), George O'Hanlon (Barney), Jerry Barclay (Jerry), Judy Harriet (young girl singer).

The Credits

Director Howard W. Koch, *Producer* Aubrey Schenck, *Screenplay* Arnold Belgard, *Story* Henrik Vollaerts, *Director of Photography* Carl E.

Guthrie, *Art Director* Robert Kinoshita, *Sound* Frank Webster, Sr., *Editor* Sam Waxman, *Music* Les Baxter. B&W 79 min. Bel-Air, released through United Artists.

Sources

Boxoffice, Vol. 73, No. 9, June 23, 1958, pg. 4.

Carnival Rock (1957)

Exploited as a rock and roll movie — *The whole tempestuous story of today's Rock 'n' Rollers told the way they want it told!* — *Carnival Rock* had little to do with rock 'n' roll except for the musical interludes, and nothing at all to do with teenagers. It was instead a grim melodrama about an older man's obsession with a younger woman. Produced and directed by Roger Corman, the film was based on a half-hour teleplay that appeared on TV's "Climax" series, written by Leo Lieberman. A prolific filmmaker, Corman hopped from genre to genre in the 1950s, establishing a reputation as the fastest director in town. Shooting began on May 15, 1957, and finished seven days later. "I don't remember it at all," Corman told Ed Naha in Naha's complimentary book about Corman, brazenly titled *Brilliance on a Budget*. "It was not a script I was overly fond of. We finished it and turned it over to a group of people in New Orleans. Apparently they did some pretty heavy editing after I turned it in. I was going to Europe and just gave them the film. I've never even seen it." It was originally intended for release by American International, a company Corman was often affiliated with, but it was Howco International who ended up with it.

The older man in Lieberman's story was played by a Broadway method actor named David Stewart, the source of much amusement and irritation for actor Dick Miller, Stewart's sidekick in the film. On the first day he and Stewart were rehearsing a scene when Stewart suddenly turned to Corman and said, "You know, I feel like (since he's my son, sort of) I want to hit him." Corman naturally assumed the actor intended to throw a fake punch. But instead he made contact. It was a slap, not a punch, but it hurt just the same.

"You don't have to hit me," Miller said angrily. "You can miss me by a foot and it's gonna look good."

They rehearsed the scene a few more times.

Ad for *Carnival Rock*.

Top: Susan Cabot coaxes Leon Tyler onto the floor in *Carnival Rock*. Bottom: Herb Reed, Dave Lynch, Paul Robi, Zola Taylor, and Tony Williams—The Platters.

"I don't *feel* it," Stewart said.

Corman pulled Miller to one side and said, "He wants to make physical contact, otherwise he doesn't feel it. Can he hit you on the take?"

Apparently Corman was slightly intimidated by having a Tony Award–winning actor in his little film, and Miller went along with the plan because he needed the job. The camera rolled, and Stewart delivered a slap to Miller's ear that left it ringing for months.

"There was a scene," Miller recalled, "where I was supposed to pull him away from this dressing room door and he kept pulling the knob off. And they'd hammer the knob back on and they would very patiently say, 'Doorknob's not real, Mr. Stewart. Don't pull the doorknob off. Don't try to turn it. *Make believe* you're turning it.' Never had that concept. And I'm supposed to pull him away from the door and slam him into the other wall and say, 'Leave her alone. She's no good for you.'"

But Stewart wouldn't let go of the knob, and he kept banging his head each time Miller threw him against the wall. Fed up, one of the grips hammered a two-headed nail into the wall and stood gleefully by while Corman ran the actors through the scene again. Miller slammed Stewart into the wall again and Stewart's head hit the nail. Miller saw blood on Stewart's head. "You're bleeding!" he exclaimed. Stewart seemed almost indifferent. "It's okay," he replied. "I can use the pain."

Miller recalled another incident with Stewart when Stewart and Miller's friend Jonathan Haze were doing a scene together. "He was doing a scene where he was supposed to see the girl with her boyfriend and have a heart attack. He gave Jonathan a straight pin and told him to stick him in the leg." They had to get some pliers to pull it out.

Nine musical interludes were shoehorned into the story, the performers a group of young hopefuls except for The Platters, who sang one number. The film's leading lady, Susan Cabot, performed two songs although she certainly wasn't known for her singing and this appears to be her only shot at it. She's backed by The Blockbusters, a group director Corman used again in *Rock All Night* (1957). David Houston, an RCA recording artist (RCA recordings: "Hasta Luego" and "Sugar Sweet," "Blue Prelude" and "I'll Always Have It on My Mind," "Someone Else's Arms" and "I Ain't Goin' There No More"), contributed a few songs, backed by Bob Luman's group The Shadows. Luman hailed from Nacogdoches, Texas, born April 15, 1938. Two years after this film he signed with Warner Bros. records and had one (very mild) hit record, "Let's Think About Living." He passed away in 1978.

Top: Bob Luman. Bottom: David Houston. Both performers appeared in *Carnival Rock*.

The Music

The Blockbusters: "Rock-A-Boogie."

Susan Cabot: "Ou-Shoo-Bla-D" and "There's No Place Without You" (with The Blockbusters).

David Houston: "One and Only" and "Teen Age Frankie and Johnnie" (with The Shadows). "One and Only" with "Hackin' Around" on the flipside was available on RCA Victor. "Teen Age Frankie and Johnnie" may have been released as well.

Bob Luman: "This Is the Night" and "All Night Long" (with The Shadows).

The Platters: "Remember When" available on Mercury.

"The Shadows: "The Creep."

Note: RCA recently released albums of Bob Luman and David Houston.

The Reception

"The direction does nothing to lighten the doleful story, one that would be sad if it were not so silly. You do not need much story to hold together a picture of this type, but what you have should work for the musical numbers, not against them." — *The Hollywood Reporter.*

"Film has a couple of very good performances in Susan

Cabot and Dick Miller. . . . Miss Cabot also effectively puts over several song numbers."—*Variety.*

"The story is so heavy-handed and poorly put together that it tends to suffocate even the rock-and-roll numbers that are the staple of such pictures."—*The Los Angeles Examiner.*

The Cast

Susan Cabot (Natalie Cook), Brian Hutton (Stanley), David J. Stewart (Christy Christakos), Dick Miller (Ben), Iris Adrian (Celia), Jonathan Haze (Max), Ed Nelson (Cannon), Bruno Ve Sota, Chris Alcaide (Slug), Horace Logran (M.C.), Yvonne Peattie (Mother), Gary Hunley (boy), Frankie Ray (Billy), Dorothy Neumann (Clara), Clara Andressa (cleaning lady #1), Terry Blake (cleaning lady #2), The Platters (themselves), David Houston (himself), Bob Luman and The Shadows (themselves), The Blockbusters (themselves).

The Credits

Producer-Director Roger Corman, *Screenplay* Leo Lieberman, *Director of Photography* Floyd Crosby, *Editor* Charles Gross, Jr., *Art Director* Robert Kinoshita, *Titles* Bill Martin, *Production Manager* Lou Place, *Assistant Director* Jack Bohrer, *Costumes* Margorie Corso, *Music* Walter Greene, Buck Ram. B&W 75 min. Howco International.

Sources

McCarty and McGee, *Little Shop of Horrors Book;* Naha, *Films of Roger Corman;* Nite, Norm N., *Rock On.*

College Confidential (1960)

This was another in a series of producer Al Zugsmith's efforts to keep the movie public abreast of the current scene in the school system. He exposed drug traffic in high schools in his searing *High School Confidential,* murder in the private sector in *Platinum High School,* and just prior to this film he exposed Mamie Van Doren in his comedy romp, *Sex Kittens Go to College.* Inspired by the Kinsey Report, Zugsmith returned to college to look at sex education. Faced with having to write

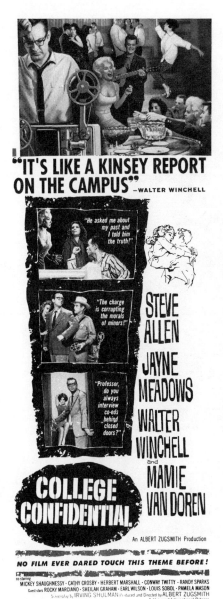

Ad for *College Confidential*.

about this film, one reviewer wanted to know if there was anything that could be done to keep Zugsmith off campus.

TV celebrity Steve Allen and his wife, Jayne Meadows, headline a typically oddball Zugsmith cast which cleverly included over a dozen press people. Allen is a sincere teacher who believes sex education ought to be taught in school (hopefully long before he should have to deal with it) and brings trouble on himself when he asks his students to participate in a sex survey. Allen gets deeper into hot water when someone slips booze into the punch at a party Allen's throwing for the kids. Allen gets drunk and watches aghast as his home movies turn into porno movies. The culprit who spiked the punch and slipped the porn movie into the show turns out to be Mickey Shaughnessy, who hoped the publicity would somehow help his daughter's acting career.

The Music

Singer Conway Twitty appeared in several Zugsmith films, though he didn't always sing in them. Twitty rose to stardom with "It's Only Make Believe," written between sets at the Flamingo Lounge in Toronto, where Twitty and his band were playing.

Mamie Van Doren and Conway Twitty goof around during a break in *College Confidential*.

In eight minutes he and Jack Nance composed the song that became one of the biggest hits of 1958 and probably the biggest hit of Twitty's career. He sounded a lot like Elvis until he moved away from rock into country, where he had a style all his own.

Twitty was from Mississippi, born in 1933, the son of a ferry boat pilot. He was named after silent actor Harold Lloyd but Twitty's manager later changed the name because he didn't think Harold Lloyd Jenkins sounded southern enough. Jenkins was headed for a career in baseball, but a draft notice queered his signing with the Philadelphia Phillies. He was stationed in Japan and began playing music in clubs. Today he still places records on the country charts.

Randy Sparks: "College Confidential," available on MGM.

Conway Twitty: "College Confidential Ball."

The Cast

Steve Allen (Steve Macinter), Jayne Meadows (Betty Duquesne), Walter Winchell (himself), Mickey Shaughnessy (Sam Grover), Cathy Crosby (Faye Grover), Herbert Marshall (Henry Addison), Conway Twitty (Marvin), Randy Sparks (Phil), Rocky Marciano (deputy sheriff), Sheilah Graham (herself), Earl Wilson (himself), Louis Sobol (himself), Pamela Mason (Edna Blake), Elisha Cook (Ted Blake), Theona Bryant (Lois Addison), Norman "Woo Woo" Grabowski (Skippy), Ziva Rodann (GoGo Lazlo), Robert Montgomery, Jr. (second boy), William Wellman, Jr. (Bob), and as themselves: Army Archerd, Jason Bacon, Nate Cutler, Nat Dallinger, Rick Du Brow, Gus Edson, Eunice Field, Joe Finnigan, Jose Haas, Harold Heffernan, Nelson Hughes, Bill Kennedy, Earl Leaf, Jack Moffitt, Lowell Redellings, Jonah Ruddy, Vernon Schott, Eve Starr, Dick Williams; and Mamie Van Doren as Sally Blake.

The Reception

"It is absurd, soggy, cheap. Why Steve Allen . . . and Jayne Meadows . . . lent their services to such an enterprise is hard to figure out." — *The Los Angeles Times.*

The Credits

Director-Producer Albert Zugsmith, *Screenplay* Irving Shulman, *Director of Photography* Carl Guthrie, A.S.C., *Editor* Edward Curtiss, *Assistant Directors* Ralph Black, Charles Scott, Jr., *Music* Dean Elliott. B&W 91 min. An Albert Zugsmith Production. A Universal-International Release.

Sources

Bronson, *Billboard Book of Number One Hits.*

Don't Knock the Rock! *(1956)*

Don't Knock was the sequel to Columbia's *Rock Around the Clock,* released earlier the same year. Like its predecessor it starred Bill Haley, whose recording of "Rock Around the Clock," a mixture of country swing and rhythm and blues, was the best-selling record of 1955. The movie grossed over $4 million, which surprised the Columbia moguls, who would have been happy with a million. They didn't realize that rock music had grabbed the souls of kids all over the United States and England, too, where teenagers danced in the streets in front of the cinemas running the movie. Occasional outbreaks of violence caused some people to wonder if the music wasn't straight from the devil's den or, at the very least, part of a Communist plot. *Don't Knock the Rock!* was Columbia's answer to those people.

In the scenario by Robert E. Kent and James B. Gordon, rock singer Arnie Haines is involved in battle against the people in his home town who want to ban rock music. Haines eventually convinces them that their reaction to rock and roll is the same as their parents' reaction to the Charleston and Black Bottom.

The choice of Alan Dale as Arnie Haines is a curious one. He'd had a mild success with "Cherry Pink and Apple Blossom White" from the motion picture *Underwater* (1955) (which actually had its premiere underwater, a wild Howard Hughes publicity stunt that was eclipsed when a young starlet hopeful named Jayne Mansfield lost her bikini top on the way out of the water). Dale's rendition of the Louiguy-David song was overtaken in popularity by Perez Prado's instrumental version. Dale wasn't a rocker, he was a crooner. He's as out of place as Buddy Holly was singing "Peggy Sue" on Arthur Murray's Dance Party TV show. Dale has five songs in the film, most of them backed by Dave Appell and His Applejacks, a somewhat uninspired group who have two numbers of their own. Shortly after *Don't Knock the Rock!* went into release Appell became an arranger-producer at Cameo Parkway records. Between his group and Dale there wasn't much room left to give the audience the kind of music they'd come for. It's doubtful that the two numbers by the Treniers helped appease anyone either.

NEWEST,
BIGGEST
ROCK 'N' ROLL
MOVIE YET!

BILL HALEY
AND HIS COMETS

Don't
Knock
The Rock

co-starring

ALAN DALE
ALAN FREED
THE TRENIERS
LITTLE RICHARD
DAVE APPELL AND HIS APPLEJACKS
with
JOVADA AND JIMMY BALLARD
Written by ROBERT E. KENT and
JAMES B. GORDON • Produced by
SAM KATZMAN • Directed by
FRED F. SEARS • A CLOVER
PRODUCTION • A COLUMBIA PICTURE

Ad for *Don't Knock the Rock!*

The Treniers were twins Claude and Cliff, their brother Buddy, Ruben Phillips (alto sax), Joe Morris, Joe Newman (both trumpets), Lucky Thompson (tenor sax), Henry "Tucker" Green (drums), Gene Gilbeaux and Don Hill and many others. Born in Mobile, Alabama, on July 14, 1919, Claude and Cliff went to Alabama State College to be teachers but were bitten by show biz after brother Buddy introduced them to the nightclub scene. Buddy'd been singing for a couple of years, and the life he was living seemed preferable to the classroom, so the twins dropped out of school. Claude got a solo gig and cut a couple of records — "I'm Gonna See My Baby" and "That Someone Must Be You" — and settled in California. Cliff went back to Mobile. Claude continued to sing in clubs around Los Angeles, then hooked up with Cliff, and they became The Trenier Twins. They, in turn, formed the Gene Gilbeaux Quartet with Gilbeaux and Hill and signed a recording contract with Mercury in 1947. As the act grew in size the name was shortened to The Treniers, and their act was said to have been full of wild Vaudevillian touches — acrobatics, humor, tap dancing, etc. Sadly the group was quite restrained in *Don't Knock the Rock!* and since their brand of music wasn't rock it's doubtful they were any more welcome than Alan Dale or the Applejacks.

Of course there were Bill Haley and His Comets, who performed six numbers, but in the few months between *Rock Around the Clock* and

Alan Dale is sandwiched between Patricia Hardy and Jana Lund. From *Don't Knock the Rock!*

The Treniers perform in *Don't Knock the Rock!*

Don't Knock the Rock! Haley had fallen out of favor with the rock and rollers, who were more attracted to the wilder, sexier and younger rockers. Thirty-year-old Haley (once known as Yodelin' Bill), with his little spit curl and his pudgy features, couldn't keep up. The only real draw the film had was Little Richard.

"I'd take one with Little Richard once a week if I could get it," said E.K. Holder, an exhibitor in Arkansas.

Disc jockey Alan Freed, who appeared in the previous film, introduced Richard in *Don't Knock the Rock!* At first the singer stood transfixed, like a toy with a dead battery, decked out in a flashy silver suit, baggy enough to house a large family. Then Richard came to life, pounding the piano keys, making suggestive hip gyrations with one leg planted on the piano lid. He was a white parent's worst nightmare come true.

Richard sang two numbers in the film, "Long Tall Sally" and "Tutti Frutti," both rock and roll classics. The songs had already been hit records prior to the release of the movie.

"Long Tall Sally," according to Robert Blackwell, who worked at Specialty Records where Richard cut his best records, was partially

Top: Little Richard and Bill Haley—*Don't Knock the Rock!* Bottom: Dave Appell and His Applejacks.

written by sixteen-year-old Enortis Johnson. The young lady walked all
the way from Mississippi to California to sell Richard a song to get
money for her sick Aunt Mary. The girl didn't have a melody, just a scrap
of paper with the following words:

> Saw Uncle John with Long Tall Sally
> They saw Aunt Mary comin'
> So they ducked back in the alley

The rest had to be improvised during the recording session.

"Tutti Frutti" was a song Richard sang when he was making twelve
bucks a week washing dishes. Whenever he wanted to say something
nasty to the boss he'd launch into awop-bop-a-loo-mop-alop-bam-boom
because the boss didn't know what that meant and neither did Richard.
The lyrics, which were shamelessly sexual, were toned down considerably by Dorothy La Bostrie, though not enough for singer Pat
Boone, the clean-cut crooner in white bucks who parents all over the
United States hoped would replace Elvis Presley. Boone changed "She
knows how to love me" to "She's a real gone cookie" and told one reporter
he didn't want to do the song in the first place. Many sources claim that
Boone's less dynamic version of the song outsold Little Richard's, which
is not unlikely, since most radio stations refused to play black recording
artists unless it was somebody who sounded white like Nat King Cole.
Yet the song is never included on the various albums of Boone's hits.

Little Richard was born Richard Wayne Penniman on December
5, 1932, in Macon, Georgia, one of twelve children. His father, a
bootlegger, kicked Richard out of the house when he found out Richard
was gay. Sixteen-year-old Richard stayed with Ann and Johnny Johnson,
owners of Macon's Tick Tock Club. Richard earned his keep by singing.
He won a talent contest in 1951 which earned him a contract with RCA.
The tracks from his two sessions there—"Get Rich Quick," "Why Did
You Leave Me," "Every Hour," "Thinkin' 'bout My Mother," "Ain't
Nothin' Happenin'," "Taxi Blues," "Please Have Mercy on Me," and "I
Brought It All on Myself"—were reissued in 1970 on RCA's low-budget
Camden label in a collection called *Every Hour with Little Richard*,
which is a pretty frightening proposal. Two of the tracks have since
resurfaced on Rhino Records' *Shut Up! A Collection of Rare Tracks,
1951–1964*. Back in 1951 the records didn't have any novelty factor and
received little notice. It wasn't until singer Lloyd Price convinced

Richard to send a demo tape to Specialty Records that things started happening for Richard. Price had given Specialty its first hit record, "Lawdy Miss Clawdy." His recommendation probably helped get Richard his audition. "Tutti Frutti" got him the contract. It became the 47th best selling song of 1956 with "Rip It Up" (with "Ready Teddy" on the flip side) right behind it at 48. "Long Tall Sally" (with "Slippin' and Slidin'" on the B-side) was ahead at 41. Then, during an outdoor concert in Sydney, Australia, Richard saw the Russian Sputnik and took it as a sign from God to quit show business. He enrolled in a bible school in Alabama and declared that rock and roll *was* the devil's music, a crushing double blow to his fans, who should have guessed that Richard would be unable to restrain himself for long. In 1963 he was back in concert with groups like The Beatles and The Rolling Stones. "The kids brought me back," Richard told biographer Charles White. "They heard the Beatles talk about me, the Stones talk about me, Tom Jones talk about me. They wanted to hear for themselves." He cut a few albums for Warner Bros., did some revival shows, always vacillating between rock and religion. He once told *Rolling Stone* magazine that two of his old sax players had died, and he interpreted their deaths as another sign from God—though the two men, Lee Allen and Alvin Tyler, were still alive. His appearance in the film *Down and Out in Beverly Hills* (1986) and his well-publicized lawsuit against Specialty returned Richard to the spotlight once again. It's amusing to see someone whose performances were often banned from radio stations, and who never was allowed on TV, in something as mainstream as a McDonald's commercial. Richard insists that he, not Elvis, is the King of Rock and Roll. At the 1988 Grammy Awards he was foolishly handed a microphone. He seized the opportunity to remind the audience that he was still waiting for *his* award. His appearance in *Don't Knock the Rock!* is one of the few records of Richard at the peak of his career.

Director Fred F. Sears was 43 when he made this movie and died a few months after its release. He'd once been a Columbia contract player,* but after a couple of years he thought he'd be better off behind

*Sears appeared in *The Locket, West of Dodge City, The Corpse Came C.O.D., Down to Earth, For the Love of Rusty, Law of the Canyon, Blondie's Anniversary* (all 1947), *Adventures in Silverado, Blondie in the Dough, Phantom Valley, Rusty Leads the Way, Whirlwind Raiders, The Gallant Blade* (all 1948), *Blazing Trail, Boston Blackie's Chinese Venture, Laramie, South of Death Valley,* and *The Lone Wolf and His Lady* (all 1949).

The incredible Leon Tyler and his partner steal the show during Bill Haley's "Rip It Up." From *Don't Knock the Rock!*

the camera and switched to directing. Most of his 48 features were made for Columbia, many for Sam Katzman. At one point in *Don't Knock the Rock!* Sears took his camera from Bill Haley and His Comets, while they sang Little Richard's "Rip It Up," to watch a bunch of teenagers dancing their hearts out. One pony-tailed lass took a rather undignified spill which remains in the film, as do gaffer's tape marks and the tracks left by the camera as it rolled away from the dancers.

"I experienced the shock of my life when I played this picture," said Harry Hawkinson, an exhibitor in Marietta, Minneapolis. The night he ran it the high school was having a play and two churches were having Lenten services. Hawkinson assumed he'd be playing to an empty house. He had the biggest crowd ever.

To insure the crowd kept coming, Columbia's ballyhoo department told the exhibitors to repeat the successful stunts used to sell the first picture in a sheet titled "Rock Showman's Honor Roll":

Radio and TV station disc jockeys, school editors, Junior Chamber of Commerce and dance school personnel invited to a screening. Omaha Theatre, Omaha, Neb.

Guest tickets to the picture awarded 25 winners of a "Name That Tune" contest on a local radio station. Riviera Theatre, St. Paul, Minn.

Disc jockey used "Mystery Tune" contest three days in advance, giving five plugs daily. Hot-rod car bannered with rock 'n' roll expressions driven around town. Cashiers answered all phone calls for two days in advance, "See You Later, Alligator!" State Theatre, Cedar Rapids, Iowa.

Supermarkets used copy in ads for six stores for two days before opening. Lyric Theatre, Duluth, Minn.

Picture ran for 36 hours continuous showing in Rock 'n' Roll Marathon, with free coffee, doughnuts and promoted record given patrons in the theatre 7 a.m. the next morning. Two papers covered story. Center Theatre, Charlotte, N.C.

Juke box promoted for free plays in the theatre lobby with special frame bearing sell copy around it. Paramount Theatre, Des Moines, Iowa.

Theatre personnel wore special beanie hats plugging the picture three weeks in advance. College Theatre, New Haven, Conn.

Television contest to find Teen King and Queen of Rock 'n' Roll, launched well in advance, with TV and radio plugs. Paramount Theatre, Kansas City, Mo.

Radio station conducted write-in contest on "What Is Rock 'n' Roll Music?" offering recordings as prizes. Alabama Theatre, Milwaukee, Wisc.

Direct broadcast of a dance hall contest to music of Bill Haley records with plugs on radio/TV. Paramount Theatre, Des Moines, Iowa.

Presidents of high school student bodies invited by phone to attend as guests. Brown Theatre, Louisville, Kentucky.

Four quiz shows on rock 'n' roll subjects held on radio show for four days with ample plugs. Student officials invited to special screening, served sandwiches and presented with record albums. Center Theatre, Oklahoma City, Okla.

Six disc jockeys on as many radio stations ran contest for entire week, using different queries. 24-sheet sound truck played recordings, visited factories, schools, neighborhood areas and downtown streets. Pilgrim Theatre, Boston, Mass.

Hotel amusement directories in 12 hotel lobbies carried plugs and playdate information. Loew's Orpheum, St. Louis, Mo.

Letter writing contest ran in two newspapers on subject of rock 'n' roll plus a panel discussion program with students and disc jockey as moderator. Strand Theatre, Portland, Maine.

Radio contest offered prizes for biggest list of Bill Haley's recordings
and a Rock 'n' Roll Dance Contest held on TV station show. Hippo-
drome Theatre, Baltimore, Md.

"This one ain't got the socko or rock 'n' roll that the first one had,"
said Colorado exhibitor Bob Walker, "but other than that, it's a pleasant
little programmer...."

The picture made money but nothing close to the original, and
Katzman concluded that rock was on the way out. His next musical was
about Calypso, and years later when a dance craze called the Twist
swept the nation, Katzman was there with *Twist Around the Clock*
(1961), a remake of *Rock Around the Clock*. And when *Twist Around the
Clock* made money, Katzman returned with — you guessed it — *Don't
Knock the Twist!*

The Music

Dave Appell and His Applejacks: "Country Dance" and "Applejack," released on Cameo Parkway. With Alan Dale: "Don't Knock the
Rock," "You're So Right," "Gonna Run," and "I Cry More."

Alan Dale: "Your Love Is My Love."

Bill Haley and His Comets: "Don't Knock the Rock," "Goofin'
Around," "Hook, Line and Sinker," "Hot Dog, Buddy, Buddy," "Calling
All Comets," and "Rip It Up," available on Decca/MCA.

Little Richard: "Long Tall Sally" and "Tutti Frutti," available on
Specialty and Rhino.

The Treniers: "Rockin' on Sunday Night" and "Out of the Bushes."

The Reception

"...a few gags and some drama, squeezed with no little effort into
a series of rock and roll numbers. Most of the lines start with the word
'man' as in 'Man, that's the craziest! Man, that's the coolest!' Etc." — *Los
Angeles Times.*

"A couple of weeks ago this reviewer spoke deprecatingly of certain aspects of the current rock and roll craze as a result of which he
was the recipient of several scolding letters.... Accordingly, it is with
some temerity that he ventures the opinion that *Don't Knock the Rock*
is not of Academy Award stature, that its story is not of Pulitzer Prize

calibre, and that its music (if that is the proper word) is sometimes uncomfortably akin to a jungle tom-tom." — *Cue.*

"A collection of top rock and roll artists have been assembled by producer Sam Katzman for his second musical in the afterbeat vein. Produced . . . for $500,000, it is packed with talent and tunes designed to appeal strongly to the juvenile trade and its prospects are bright on that reckoning." — *Variety.*

". . . a little hard to dig for anyone not in the full flush of youth. But the picture is tastefully done, with some imaginative touches." — *Box-office.*

"There seems to be a veritable spade [sic] of pictures about this thing called rock and roll (excuse it if we don't put that in caps). Obviously, these flicks are being made for one reason, to attract the youthful followers of this cult and to get all of the mileage possible out of the recording artists who are dedicated to the premise that if it ain't r&r it ain't music." — *The Los Angeles Examiner.*

". . . emulates its predecessor in every respect. The story-line is virtually non-existent, serving only to link up musical numbers." — *Monthly Film Bulletin.*

The Cast

Bill Haley and His Comets (themselves), Alan Dale (Arnie Haines), Alan Freed (himself), The Treniers (themselves), Little Richard (who else), Dave Appel and his Applejacks (themselves), Jovada and Jimmy Ballard (themselves), Patricia Hardy (Francine MacLaine), Fay Baker (Arlene MacLaine), Jana Lund (Sunny Everett), Gail Ganley (Mollie Haines), Pierre Watkin (Mayor George Bagley), George Cisar (Mayor Tom Everett), Dick Elliott (Sheriff Cagle).

The Credits

Director Fred F. Sears, *Producer* Sam Katzman, *Story & Screenplay* Robert E. Kent and James B. Gordon, *Director of Photography* Benjamin H. Kline, *Assistant Director* Sam Nelson, *Art Director* Paul Palmentola, *Editor* Edwin Bryant, A.C.E., and Paul Borofsky, *Set Decorator* Sidney Clifford, *Choreographer* Earl Barton, *Sound* Josh Westmoreland, *Musical Supervisor* Fred Karger. B&W 84 min. Columbia.

Sources

Boxoffice Vol. 70, No. 15, February 2, 1957, pg. 11; Vol. 70, No. 25, April 13, 1957, pg. 11; Vol. 71, No. 5, May 25, 1957, pg. 11; Vol. 71, No. 6, June 1, 1957, pg. 13; Vol. 71, No. 17, August 17, 1957, pg. 11; Vol. 71, No. 24, October 12, 1957, pgs. 12, 13; Pareles and Romanowski, *Rolling Stone Encyclopedia of Rock & Roll*; Stambler, *Encyclopedia of Pop Rock and Soul*; White, *Life and Times of Little Richard*.

Frankenstein's Daughter (1958)

This weak flop does not seem to evoke a pleasant nostalgia as do many awful sci fi films from the fifties. It couldn't have been less horrifying. The exteriors were shot around the producer's home; the laboratory set was dressed with junked props loaned for the cost of the repair.

"I knew when we were making the film that it didn't seem very frightening," said John Ashley, who starred in the film opposite Sandra Knight, Jack Nicholson's first wife. "There I was with this table between me and this monster and I'm rocking it back and forth and I couldn't believe that what we were doing was going to somehow be terrifying because it was on a big screen. It could only be worse. I say this to you now, in retrospect, but these are not thoughts I would have shared at the time. You don't want to hurt anyone's feelings. The fellow that directed that film was doing his best. But when you don't have any time and you don't have any money there's only so much you can do no matter how talented you are."

The Music

Page Cavanaugh and His Trio (featuring Harold Lloyd, Jr.): "Special Date," recently released on Rhino.

The Reception

"The conception throughout is naive and crude, while the almost incredibly weak performance by Felix Locher as an elderly, well-meaning scientist adds an unintentionally humorous note."—*Monthly Film Bulletin.*

". . . it's a toss-up whether [*Frankenstein's Daughter* or its cofeature]

Missile to the Moon is the cheaper, duller piece of claptrap." — *New York Times.*

". . . a dismal clinker . . ." — *The Los Angeles Examiner.*

". . . one of the worst films ever made." — Bill Warren, *Keep Watching the Skies!*

"Holds up." — Mark McGee.

The Cast

Donald Murphy (Oliver Frankenstein), Sandra Knight (Trudy Norton), Felix Locher (Uncle Carter), Wolfe Barzel (Elsu), John Ashley (Johnny Bruder), Sally Todd (Suzie Lawler), Harold Lloyd, Jr. (Don), John Zaremba (Lt. Boyle), Robert Dix (Detective Dillon), Viktaure Oerjubs (chemist), Harry Wilson (monster), Bill Coontz and George Barrows (warehousemen).

The Credits

Director Richard Cunha, *Producer* Marc Frederic, *Screenplay* H.E. Barrie, *Art Director* Sham Unlimited, *Director of Photography* Meredith Nicholson, *Editor* Everett Dodd, *Sound* Robert Post, *Assistant Director* Leonard J. Shapiro, *Music* Nicholas Carras.

Source

Warren, *Keep Watching the Skies!*

The Giant Gila Monster (1958)

This one was released as a package with *The Killer Shrews*, the first productions from McClendon Radio Pictures. Gordon McClendon owned a large ranch in Texas where various film companies and would-be filmmakers came to shoot their movies. It wasn't long before McClendon decided to get into production himself. He'd written a number of radio spots of American International, so he was familiar with their combination packages, which he copied. He chose to make what was considered at the time the easiest type of film to market — science fiction. Reportedly, *Gila Monster* cost $138,000 to make and was originally budgeted at $300,000. More likely it cost under $100,000 and

Don Sullivan sings "The Mushroom Song" (top) while the Giant Gila Monster lurks outside (bottom).

in all probability the $300,000 figure was the original estimate for the whole double-feature package.

The star of the film is Don Sullivan, who had a brief career in low-budget films during the late fifties and early sixties. He plays Chase Winstead, a good-hearted teenager who works at an auto repair place to earn enough money to support his crippled sister. In between pounding fenders and lube jobs he finds the time to build his own hot rod and write rock and roll songs. A chance encounter with disc jockey Steamroller Smith (Ken Knox) of station KILT (a Houston radio station owned by McClendon) starts Chase on his way to a successful recording career. He's in the middle of a song at a local record hop, hosted by Steamroller Smith, when the gila monster (which has been troublesome throughout the picture) bursts into the place. Chase loads nitroglycerin into his prize hot rod and sends it crashing into the big lizard, blowing it and his hot rod to bits.

The Music

Don Sullivan: "The Mushroom Song" and "My Baby She Rocks."

The Reception

"It seems that a big theater exhibitor in Dallas got together some money and after bowing three times in the direction of Hollywood (the producing company is actually called Hollywood Pictures Corp.) turned out these features. They're not very much, I'm afraid." — *Los Angeles Examiner.*

"Don Sullivan is adequate as the male lead; he uses the appearance to exploit three of his own compositions. A dubious interpolation. His vocal assets don't match even his minor acting talents." — *Variety.*

"Sullivan, whose work we have noted before, is personable, a soft-spoken and rather skilled young actor, who must graduate from these little efforts some time soon." — *Los Angeles Times.*

The Cast

Don Sullivan (Chase Winstead), Fred Graham (sheriff), Lisa Simone (Lisa), Shug Fisher (Harris), Bob Thompson (Wheeler), Janice Stone (Missy), Ken Knox (Steamroller Smith), Jerry Cortwright (Bob), Beverly Thurman (Gay), Don Flournoy (Gordy), Clarke Brown

(Chuck), Pat Simmons (Sherry), Pat Reeves (Rick), Ann Sonka (Whila), Cecil Hunt (Compton), Tommie Russel (Blackwell), Grady Vaughn (Pat Wheeler), Yolanda Salas (Liz Humphries), Howard Ware (Eb Humphries), Stormy Meadows (Agatha Humphries), Desmond Dough (hitchhiker), Gay and Jan McLendon.

The Credits

Director-Story-Special Effects Ray Kellogg, *Producer* Ken Curtis, *Screenplay* Jay Simms, *Executive Producer* Gordon McLendon, *Director of Photography* Wilfrid Cline, *Editor* Aaron Snell, *Sound* Earl Snyder, *Assistant Director* Edward Haldeman, *Music* Jack Marshall.

The Girl Can't Help It (1956)

The Girl combined rock music with another 1950's phenomenon, blonde bombshell Jayne Mansfield. Obviously 20th Century–Fox had more faith in the actress than in the music, for nearly every performance is interrupted to give Miss Mansfield another chance to thrust her bountiful chest across the CinemaScope screen. "Her breasts were fifty inches and she didn't wear a brassiere," said Little Richard to author Charles White, although most accounts of Jayne's measurements have them at forty-one inches.

"Miss Mansfield drew the usual cat-calls and whistles," said Michigan exhibitor F.A. Phillips, "but it was the music they came for." Most of his fellow exhibitors agreed, but they all tipped their hats to Fox for giving the men a little something extra to look at. One chap claimed he was so mesmerized by Jayne's measurements he "plumb forgot to change the reels."

Frank Tashlin, the director of the film, once remarked that there was nothing funnier to him than a big-breasted woman, and he took every opportunity to tickle his own funnybone. In scene after scene references are made to Miss Mansfield's bazooms. Ice melts, eyeglasses shatter and milk boils out of bottles as she walks by, her chest barely contained by the screen. Even Tashlin was taken aback when the actress stepped into his office for the first time in her tight-fitting, striped sweater. He thought her chest was fake until she pulled her sweater off.

Born Vera Jayne Palmer in 1933, Mansfield spent her childhood in a middle class neighborhood in Phillipsburg, New Jersey. Her father

Ad for *The Girl Can't Help It.*

Jayne Mansfield is getting instructions from gangster Edmond O'Brien and Tom Ewell hopes she won't listen. From *The Girl Can't Help It.*

died when she was a child, leaving her overly strict mother to raise her. Jayne would often gaze at the dusty summer road in front of her house and imagine a handsome knight coming to her rescue. She settled for Paul Mansfield, who married her at fourteen and took her to California. After calling every agent in the phone book and having little success, Jayne called the studios herself and got an audition at Paramount but not a job. A photographer named Frank Worth told her about a little ten-day picture called *Hangover,* for which she earned $200 a week. A few days into the production the leading lady left the project for a better part in a live television drama and the script was quickly re-written to more heavily feature Jayne's character. It was a lucky break for the distributor, but not the producer, who'd peddled the film to every studio in town before a little independent outfit took it on. By that time Jayne Mansfield had been the subject of hundreds of magazine and newspaper articles. *Time* ran a picture of her with the caption "Sex on the rocks!" which the distributor wisely quoted in the advertisements for the film, which was released as *Female Jungle* (1956). Jayne was signed at Warner Bros. but played only bits until the studio loaned her to an independent outfit for the lead in *The Burglar* (1955). During the production Warner Bros. let her option drop. As a consolation her agent got her the lead in a Broadway play, *Will Success Spoil Rock Hunter?* which ran 452 performances. Fox bought the play and gave Jayne a contract as a way of keeping Marilyn Monroe in line. Monroe was the studio's hottest property, but she was starting to want more say in the roles she played. Signing Jayne was Fox's way of reminding Monroe there was more than one sexy bimbo in the bush, although great pains were taken to portray Jayne as something other than a bimbo. A four-part profile in the Hearst newspapers that ran in conjunction with the release of *TGCHI* made note of Jayne's extremely high I.Q. and her interest in the violin. But her cleavage was her trademark.

"...Tashlin has focussed so much emphasis on Jayne's fabled perimeters as to make many in the audience lose sight of the fine performances given to the Messrs. Ewell and O'Brien," wrote the critic for the *Los Angeles Examiner*. And sandwiched between her breasts was a lot of great music by people like the already mentioned Little Richard, Fats Domino, Eddie Cochran, Gene Vincent and The Platters. Edmond O'Brien, an Academy Award winner not known for his singing, does a spirited number called "Rock Around the Rock Pile," also performed by Ray Anthony. Anthony's appearance in the film was ironic as his career was on the decline, which he blamed on rock music. A trumpet player since childhood, Anthony had his own band by 1946 and had his first hit record shortly after signing with Capitol in 1950. He's best known for his pop versions of "Dragnet" and "Peter Gunn." His stormy marriage to actress Mamie Van Doren (another platinum sexpot) led to a brief acting career.

Other performers included The Chuckles, The Treniers, Johnny Oleen, Abbey Lincoln, and Eddie Fontaine singing "Cool It Baby," the song, from Fox's *Teenage Rebel* (1956).

Nino Tempo, a singer with Benny Goodman's orchestra at eight, did "Tempo's Tempo" in the film. In 1963 Tempo and his sister, April Stevens, recorded a series of updated classics like "Deep Purple" and "Whispering" for Atco. (Your author most fondly remembers their version of "I Love How You Love Me" with a bagpipe interlude.)

Julie London made a brief appearance to sing her biggest hit record, "Cry Me a River." Her first screen role was in *Nabonga* (1944) as a jungle princess. Born in Santa Clara, California, she married actor-director Jack Webb and was later the star of Webb's "Emergency" TV

Little Richard (top) and Eddie Cochran (bottom) in *The Girl Can't Help It*.

series co-starring her second husband, Bobby Troup. (Troup wrote the title song for *The Girl Can't Help It*.) London wasn't a major star but was quite good and sensual in films like *Man of the West* (1957) and *Wonderful Country* (1959).

Jayne Mansfield made a few more movies for Fox, but by 1963 her career had sagged to the point that she had to appear buck naked to get a part in a black and white cheapie called *Promises! Promises!* She was killed in the summer of 1967 when she crashed into the back of a parked truck. When she first came to Hollywood she stood on the corner of Sunset and Vine and knew the town would ultimately belong to her. Seventeen years later she'd seen her best years come and go. She'd become a parody of a parody. Writers have often depicted her as another Hollywood tragedy, used and tossed aside like a paper cup. Then again, where else but in Hollywood could you become a star, however briefly, just by having humongous hooters?

The Music

Ray Anthony: "Rock Around the Rock Pile," released on Capital with "Big Band Boogie."
The Chuckles: "Cinnamon Sinner."
Eddie Cochran: "20 Flight Rock," released on Liberty.
Fats Domino: "Blue Monday," released on Imperial.
Eddie Fontaine: "Cool It Baby," released on Decca.
Julie London: "Cry Me a River" (Liberty).
Abbey Lincoln: "Spread the Word" (Liberty).
Johnny Oleen: "I Ain't Gonna Cry No More" and "My Idea of Love" (Liberty).
The Platters: "You'll Never, Never Know" (Mercury).
Nino Tempo: "Tempo's Tempo" (Liberty).
The Treniers: "Rockin' Is Our Bizness."
Gene Vincent: "Be Bop a Lula" (Capitol).

The Reception

"A rock-and-roll comedy with class . . . as effervescent as New Year's Eve and as goofy and gay as somebody else's funny paper hat."— *The Hollywood Reporter*.

"This was even more than they could have asked for—color,

CinemaScope, good stars, with Jayne Mansfield to hold the men's attention. Fellow exhibitors, do not miss showing this one. It's the most!" — Jerry Walden, a Texas exhibitor.

"It is an hilarious comedy with a beat, and the younger set will take to it like a double malt and cheeseburger. . . . Miss Mansfield doesn't disappoint as the sexpot. . . . Nature was so much more bountiful with her than with Marilyn Monroe that it seems Miss Mansfield should have left MM with her voice." — *Variety.*

"This is the best of the rock and roll pictures. I advertised this weeks ahead as the one Princess Margaret enthusiastically clapped and jogged to when she saw it, thereby appealing to the middle-aged patrons and the toffee-noses!" — Dave Klein, a Northern Rhodesia exhibitor.

"The picture kids sex frankly and unabashedly. It pokes fun at the shimmier and shadier aspects of the aboriginal contortions of the current rock and roll set; and takes a good-natured swipe at movie mobsters and fast-talking talent agents who live hand-to-mouth until they can latch onto a nice ten per cent payoff." — *Cue.*

"Instead of a horde of frantic teenagers expressing themselves we have Miss Mansfield expressing herself in this rock and roll opus. Somehow, she makes the big beat sound better." — *Los Angeles Mirror News.*

The Cast

Tom Ewell (Tom Miller), Jayne Mansfield (Jerri Jordan), Edmond O'Brien (Marty "Fats" Murdock, King of the Slots), Julie London (herself), Ray Anthony (himself), Barry Gordon (himself), Henry Jones (Mousie), John Emery ("Legs" Wheeler), Juanita Moore (Hilda), Fats Domino (himself), The Platters (themselves), Little Richard (himself), Gene Vincent (himself), The Blue Caps (themselves), The Treniers (themselves), Eddie Fontain (himself), The Chuckles (themselves), Johnny Oleen (himself), Abbey Lincoln (herself), Nino Tempo (himself), Eddie Cochran (himself).

The Credits

Producer-Director Frank Tashlin, *Screenplay* Frank Tashlin and Herbert Baker, *Story* Garson Kanin, *Music* Lionel Newman, *Director of*

Photography Leon Shamroy, A.S.C., *Art Directors* Lyle R. Wheeler and
Leland Fuller, *Set Decorators* Walter M. Scott and Paul S. Fox, *Special
Effects* Ray Kellogg, *Editor* James B. Clark, A.C.E., *Costumes* Charles
LeMaire, *Makeup* Ben Nye, S.M.A., *Hair* Helen Turpin, C.H.S., *Sound*
E. Clayton Ward and Harry M. Leonard, *Assistant Director* Ad
Schaumer. C/CS 96 min. 20th Century–Fox.

Sources

Boxoffice, Vol. 70, No. 20, March 9, 1957, pg. 7; Vol. 71, No. 4,
May 18, 1957, pg. 11; Dowdy, *Films of the Fifties;* Luijters and Timmer,
Life and Death of Jayne Mansfield; Peary, *Cult Movies;* White, *Life and
Times of Little Richard.*

Girls Town (1959)

In this variation of *Boys Town*, Maggie Hayes takes Spencer Tracy's
part and Mamie Van Doren gets the Mickey Rooney role. Elinor Donahue (Princess on "Father Knows Best") is Mamie's sister. At the beginning of the film she kills a boy in self-defense. Hot rodder Mel Torme
saw the whole thing but threatens to tell the police otherwise unless Elinor agrees to join a vice ring in Mexico. Mamie busts out of Girls Town
with help from Gloria Talbott and exposes the truth. According to Miss
Van Doren, Cardinal Spellman thought she exposed a little too much.
Since the film concerned the Catholic Church, producer Albert Zugsmith took the final cut to Spellman for his approval. His Holiness disap-
proved of Mamie's bare shoulders in a shower scene. "But your grace,"
Zugsmith said, "even *bad* girls take showers." The scene was snipped.

The Music

Paul Anka sings one of his biggest records, "Lonely Boy." He was
only 18 when he made this picture and was already one of the most successful singer-songwriters in the business.

Born July 30, 1941, in Ottawa, Canada, Anka was 15 when his song
to his 18-year-old babysitter, "Diana," hit the top of the charts. "Lonely
Boy" was written after his mother's death from a bad liver. In the late
fifties Anka was rarely off the charts. He still has a hit now and then,
but mostly he writes hits for other singers. Sinatra's "My Way" and

Ad for *Girls Town.*

Tom Jones' "She's a Lady" were both his. He gets $30,000 a year in royalties for his "Tonight Show" theme.

The Platters do one number, staged to conceal the fact that lead singer Tony Williams was no longer with the group.

Paul Anka: "Lonely Boy," "A Time to Cry," "Girls Town" (with Mamie Van Doren), and "Ave Maria." The first two songs are available on ABC-Paramount.

Cathy Crosby: "I Love You."

Mamie Van Doren: "Hey, Mama."

The Platters: "Wish It Were Me."

The Reception

". . . expertly geared for young audiences . . ."—*The Hollywood Reporter.*

"A highlight of the film naturally are the songs of the popular Anka."—*Film Daily.*

". . . it is a blatantly crude and vulgar film. There is a patina of fake piety spread over some of the proceedings by putting part of the action at an institution run by Catholic nuns. This won't fool the prurient-minded, although it could easily be offensive to Catholics."—*Variety.*

Mel Torme and Elinor Donahue in *Girls Town*.

The Cast

Mamie Van Doren (Silver Morgan), Mel Torme (Fred Alger), Paul Anka (Jimmy Parlow), Ray Anthony (Dick Culdane), Maggie Hayes (Mother Veronica), Cathy Crosby (singer), Gigi Perreau (Serafina Garcia), Elinor Donahue (Mary Lee Morgan), Gloria Talbott (Vida), Sheilah

Graham (Sister Grace), Jim Mitchum (Charley Boy), Dick Contino (Stan Joyce), Harold Lloyd, Jr. (Chip Gardner), Charles Chaplin, Jr. (Joe Cates), Peggy Moffit (Flo), Jody Fair (Gloria Barker), Peter Leeds (Michael Clyde), Nan Peterson (carhop), Woo Woo Grabrowski ("Skin"), Karen Von Unge (Sister Agnes), Susanne Sydney (Carlie), Nancy Root (Jaguar girl), Wendy Wilde (Sister Magdalen), Bobi Byrnes (Dolores), Gloria Rhoads (matron), Phyllis Douglas (Eleanor).

The Credits

Director Charles Haas, *Producer* Albert Zugsmith, *Screenplay* Robert Smith, *Story* Robert Hardy Andrews, *Director of Photography* John L. Russell, *Art Director* Hans Peters and Jack T. Collis, *Sound* Franklin Milton, *Editor* Leon Barsha, *Music* Van Alexander. B&W 92 min. An Albert Zugsmith Production. A Metro-Goldwyn-Mayer Presentation.

Sources

Bronson, *Billboard Book of Number One Hits;* Van Doren, *Playing the Field.*

Go, Johnny, Go! (1959)

The saga of disc jockey Alan Freed continues. This was one of two movies Hal Roach, Jr., contracted Freed to make. But Roach's company went belly-up before Freed could make *The Alan Freed Rock 'n' Roll Story.* This picture was originally called *The Singing Story of Johnny Rock and Roll.*

As always, Freed played himself, a tireless rock music crusader. In this episode Freed hangs around a lot with Chuck Berry. Berry's excited by Freed's new discovery, Johnny Melody. Freed bends Berry's ear with a lengthy account of how the boy entered one of Freed's talent contests and how winning stopped the boy from becoming a juvenile delinquent.

The troubled boy is played by Jimmy Clanton, an unusually cleancut choice for Freed, who refused to play Pat Boone's records on his radio program. Clanton was a Louisiana boy, only eighteen when he made this movie (born September 2, 1940). His first hit was "Just a Dream" in 1958. Although the title song of *Go, Johnny, Go!* (which is "Johnny B. Goode") is sung by Chuck Berry, Clanton had a hit the year this film was released called "Go, Jimmy, Go."

The Music

Especially noteworthy is a rare screen appearance by Ritchie Valens, recently the subject of a screen biography starring Lou Diamond Phillips, *La Bamba* (1987). Valens was one of the three singers immortalized by a fatal plane crash that also killed Buddy Holly and Jape "The Big Bopper" Richardson, the only one who hasn't had a biography made of his short life. Valens was the first Chicano rock star. His real name was Valenzuela and he grew up poor in Pacoima, California. He died February 3, 1959, just prior to the release of this film.

Also appearing in Freed's lineup was another singer from the poor side of town, Jackie Wilson, once introduced by bumbling Ed Sullivan as a young man out of Detroit. Said Sullivan: "I suppose there's no performer of his race who is as well beloved by his own people and by record fans everywhere." Wilson sang "Lonely Teardrops" on Sullivan's show that night, his bestselling record. He was singing it again in 1975 when a stroke left him in a heap on the stage. The audience, thinking it was part of the act, applauded. Wilson was known for wild splits and fancy footwork, things he'd learned as a boxer.

Ad for *Go, Johnny, Go!*

Top: (Left–right) Chuck Berry, Sandy Stewart, and Alan Freed. Bottom: Harvey Fuqua, one of The Moonglows.

Eddie Cochran in his final film appearance — *Go, Johnny, Go!*

One night he deliberately whipped an audience into a frenzy so they wouldn't notice headliner Roy Hamilton hadn't shown. After flirting with his audience for an hour or so Wilson jumped into the middle of it. Women tore off his clothes before the police extracted him. One female fan wanted him so badly she came to his apartment at four in the morning and threatened to kill herself with a gun if he didn't show her

some attention. But it was Wilson who caught two bullets in his belly.
A few years later his affair with Playboy bunny Karen Lynn Calloway
came to a nasty conclusion when the woman's husband pumped five
slugs into her. Wilson died in 1984. He had a terrific voice usually
wasted on ballads but now and then he'd dip into the blues and give
everyone a treat.

In *Rhythm and Blues,* author Lynn McCutcheon asked black
singers if they thought the church had any influence on their music. The
response was unanimous—the church *was* the roots. "It's all spiritual
roots," said singer Archie Bell, "and a lot of rhythm and blues things are
taken from church songbooks." And it was church music that moved
Chuck Berry. Berry recalled for McCutcheon a hymn that repeated the
word "walk" several times, and each time the word was said, the
deacons tapped the wooden floor. "It jarred the whole church and got
into me that vibration from the floor," recalled Berry. Two years later,
with the vibration still in him, he began singing in the choir of the An-
tioch Baptist Church in Missouri and later taught himself to play the
guitar while he was in high school. He joined Johnny Johnson's Trio, but
their gig at the Cosmopolitan Club in East St. Louis didn't pay enough
to support his wife and two kids so he took a second job on a General
Motors assembly line. Muddy Waters saved him from that dreary endeavor by introducing him to Phil and Leonard Chess, a couple of
brothers who specialized in rhythm and blues records. The Chess
brothers knew the real money was in the white rock and roll market.
They picked Berry because he sounded white. His first record,
"Maybellene" (actually a version of an old country song called "Ida
Red"), broke into the top ten. You'll find Alan Freed's name on the
record as one of its writers, a gesture that enabled Freed to collect a
percentage of the sales (money that wouldn't quite look so much like
the bribe it was so that Freed would give the record a lot of air play).
Freed promised to give Berry back his share of the credit during a
drunken moment at a party but never made good the promise. It took
Berry over a decade through litigation to set things right again. Berry
was one of the few singers to look out for himself in the legal department.

"It was during the filming of *Go, Johnny, Go!* . . . that I realized
what a heavy drinker Alan was," Berry remarked in his autobiography.
"It seemed at first he could hold his take as well as Johnnie Johnson
could, without it affecting his ability to perform his professional ob-
ligations. But just since I had known him, I could notice the physical

deterioration of his body under the quantity of alcohol I assumed he was consuming."

Berry worked for five days at the Hal Roach Studio in Culver City. He continued to tour until March 1960, when he was sentenced to five years' imprisonment for taking a white prostitute across state borders. The music scene took a decidedly different turn while Berry was behind bars. A Senate subcommittee made rock music very undesirable by exposing the bribes, planting the suggestion that if you played rock music, you were on the take. Disc jockeys looked for less offensive music, and by the end of the year the top ten sounded pretty much the way it had when the decade began.

Chuck Berry: "Memphis, Tennessee" and "Little Queenie," available on Chess.

The Cadillacs: "Jay Walker" and "Please Mr. Johnson."

Jo Ann Campbell: "Mama, Can I Go Out."

Jimmy Clanton: "Angel Face," "Once Again," "My Love Is Strong," "Now the Day Is Over," "It Takes a Long, Long Time," "Ship on a Stormy Sea," and "You Done Me Wrong" (with Sandy Stewart).

Eddie Cochran: "Teenage Heaven," available on Liberty.

The Flamingos: "Jump Children."

Harvey: "Don't Be Afraid to Love."

Sandy Stewart: "Playmates" and "Heavenly Father."

Richard Valens: "Oh! My Head!"

Jackie Wilson: "You'd Better Know It," available on Rhino.

The Reception

". . . this dreadfully noisy production has a total of 19 not altogether musical numbers, which adds up to close to a full hour devoted to rock and roll and leaves very little time for story." — *The Los Angeles Times.*

"The main thing the picture points up is the loudness and sameness to the r&r beat. Also, it's an asset for the singers to be acrobats." — *The Los Angeles Examiner.*

The Cast

Alan Freed (himself), Jimmy Clanton (Johnny Melody), Sandy Stewart (Julie), Chuck Berry (himself), Herb Vigran (Bill Barnett), Frank Wilcox (Mr. Arnold), Barbara Woodell (Mrs. Arnold), Milton

Frome (Mr. Martin), Joe Cranston (band leader), Inga Boling (secretary).

The Credits

Director Paul Landres, *Producers* Hal Roach, Jr., and Alan Freed, *Screenplay* Gary Alexander, *Director of Photography* Ed Fitzgerald, *Art Director* McClure Capps, *Editor* Walter Hannemann, *Sound* Charles Althouse, *Music* Leon Klatzkin.

Sources

Berry, *Chuck Berry;* Miller, *Rolling Stone Illustrated History of Rock & Roll.*

High School Confidential (1958)

This film continued the Hollywood tradition of spreading misinformation about marijuana that had begun with films like *Reefer Madness* and *Assassin of Youth* back in the 1930s. Albert Zugsmith, once a line producer at Universal-International, left the studio in 1958 and signed a multi-picture deal at MGM. Joseph Vogel, the president of Loew's Inc., said it marked "the latest step in the studio's aggressive policy of bringing top creative talents into the company." Zugsmith's name was on some of U-I's most profitable and respected movies — *Written on the Wind, The Incredible Shrinking Man, Touch of Evil.* What Vogel didn't realize was Zugsmith had been restraining himself during his five years with Universal. And *High School Confidential* was only a hint of things to come.

Zugsmith was born on April 24, 1910, in Atlantic City, New Jersey, and became the publisher of the city's *Daily News.* He entered show business in 1953, made a couple of low-budget movies and signed a contract to produce films at Universal. It was there that he met actress Mamie Van Doren, one of the stars of *High School Confidential,* and the film's director, Jack Arnold, who later confessed that he was not at all happy with Zugsmith. Arnold remarked that Zugsmith was a man of "extreme bad taste," always "happiest when the films were the nastiest." Zugsmith's later films, which he directed himself, seem to validate Arnold's assessment. Films such as *Confessions of an Opium Eater* virtually wallow in sleaze and slime, incoherent at best, ugly at worst.

Two ads for *High School Confidential*.

Russ Tamblyn as Tony Baker/Mike Wilson in Zugsmith's classic *High School Confidential*.

Fortunately, Zugsmith was still exercising some semblance of discretion when he made *High School Confidential*, and Arnold's direction is crisp. Unlike most juvenile delinquency films, it's never boring.

"I don't make movies without a moral," said Zugsmith, "but you can't make a point for good unless you expose the evil!" Zugsmith claimed his movie was "true-to-life," and he took pains to make it that way. He hired character actor Mel Welles, something of a beatnik, to supply writers Lewis Meltzer and Robert Blees with a lot of jive talk. One critic noted there was so much "hipster talk it could . . . be said the film might well be equipped with English subtitles." Zugsmith did the next best thing by compiling a "DIGtionary" with over 100 hip-talk phrases as a promotional gimmick.

Seventeen-year-old Kathleen Briggs was also hired by Zugsmith, but the exact nature of her contribution wasn't stated in the newspaper account of her $9000 lawsuit against the producer. The young lady claimed she was to be employed as an actress and tour with the film for a total of twelve weeks at $750 a week as payment for the material she supplied.

The idea for the film began with a newspaper story about the son of a Texas Ranger who infiltrated a drug ring to gather evidence and was murdered. Other incidents in the Meltzer-Blees scenario were obtained through conversations with young marijuana addicts.

Russ Tamblyn was chosen to play the part of the undercover agent. He was in England, working on *tom thumb,* when MGM notified him that his date to begin his tour of duty in the army had been postponed a few weeks so he could be in Zugsmith's film. Returning to the States, Tamblyn was met at the airport by Zugsmith, who hustled him to the studio's wardrobe department, then drove him to a hotel in Brentwood, handed him a copy of the script, and told him to report for work the next morning.

"It was the first time I'd seen the script," Tamblyn recalled. "After I read it I said to myself, 'Oh, man, what a piece of crap!' I called my agent and told him I didn't want to do it. He told me the studio would suspend me if I didn't. That was that. I'd been nominated for my role in *Peyton Place* and when I attended the ceremony I sat there thinking: Here I was in this big, big movie and I'm doing this thing with Mamie Van Doren. I couldn't believe it."

Regardless of his feelings, Tamblyn was excellent in the picture. The film opens with the grim face of Dr. Stewart Knox, chairman of the Los Angeles County Medical Association Narcotics Committee. Knox asks the audience: "How many parents are awake to the temptations facing their children? I do not mean petty infringements. I refer to the terribly dangerous traffic which this film exposes. The story takes place in America, but it could happen anywhere, which is why police throughout the world have special divisions in close international cooperation to deal with this modern problem. *High School Confidential* will shock you and, I hope, alert you."

The next thing the audience sees is rock 'n' roller Jerry Lee Lewis, riding on the back of a flatbed truck, pounding away at his piano, singing the film's title song. After which Tamblyn arrives on the scene and immediately causes trouble, first by bullying his way into a parking space, then by making an obnoxious pass at the first cute young lady he sees. "Hi ya, sexy," he says, "You look real cultured. Let's cut out to some drag 'n' eat pad." He later makes good his boast that by the end of the day, the whole crummy school would know who he was. This he accomplishes by pulling a knife on three tough cats and insulting his history teacher and his principal. A few loose remarks about "looking to graze on some grass" nets Tamblyn the drug connection he's after, who takes him to Mister A (Jackie Coogan), the top man whom Tamblyn ultimately brings to justice.

Anticipating trouble over depicting youths taking drugs, Zugsmith sought to squelch the idea that he'd produced the picture for sensational reasons by calling a press conference. He told the reporters that *High School Confidential* was very much in the spirit of his own *Slaughter on 10th Avenue,* a picture of a crusading nature. The conditions outlined in *HSC* did exist and unless exposed could spread like wildfire. Unlike *Blackboard Jungle,* Zugsmith pointed out, his film had a clear-cut moral lesson. Yet the radio spots for the picture compared it to *Blackboard Jungle:*

ANNOUNCER: MGM presents *High School Confidential,* a shattering drama about the rock 'n' roll world of today's teen-agers! Not since *Blackboard Jungle* has the shocking picture of these untamed teens been so violently revealed. *High School Confidential* shows you the truth about their torrid temptations—their violence, speed and ruthless terror. A rocking . . . hopping . . . shocking picture of the dangerous truth you never dreamed existed! Find out for yourself what the tough troubled teenagers of our times are like. See Russ Tamblyn, Jan Sterling, John Drew Barrymore, Diane Jergens and the new singing sensation of our teenagers—Jerry Lee Lewis.

Sheet music for the *High School Confidential* theme song, featuring The Killer himself—Jerry Lee Lewis.

"Just point me at the piano, and give me my money and in fifteen minutes I'll have 'em shaking, shouting, shivering, and shaking," Lewis told a reporter from the *Los Angeles Times.*

Jerry Lee Lewis was the son of Elmo and Mamie Lewis, born September 20, 1935, in Ferriday, Louisiana. Legend has it that he was beating pianos to death when he was only nine. "I taught myself everything about the piano," he told the *Times.* "I wasn't influenced by anyone. I lived so far back in the country, I don't think I knew anyone who could influence me." His father used to drive him to neighboring towns and just like in *High School Confidential,* Jerry would play piano from the back of the flatbed truck. By 1956, when he and his father took the family's battered old Chevy to Sun Records to cut a demo, Jerry'd been married twice and jailed once. "Crazy Arms," his first Sun single, sold reasonably well, but it was "Whole Lot of Shakin' Going On" that did the trick. Sam Phillips, the owner of Sun Records, didn't think the song had much of a chance because of its highly suggestive lyrics. Phillips' energies went into promoting the flip side, "It'll Be Me," written by Jack Clement during a particularly rough bowel movement. "If you see a turd in your toilet bowl, baby it'll be me and I'll be starin' at you" was changed to, "If you see a lump of sugar in your sugar bowl, it'll be me and I'll be looking at you." But it was "Shakin'" that caught fire, especially after Phillips' brother Jud took Jerry to New York and introduced him to Jules Green, Steve Allen's manager. Jerry's appearance on Steve Allen's Sunday night TV show sent the song through the roof. Allen couldn't resist making fun of Lewis, first with a silly introduction and later by throwing furniture past the camera when the singer broke loose. Allen poked fun at rock music on his program all of the time, routinely reading rock lyrics the way Charles Laughton read poetry. But Allen booked rockers that no one else would touch, at least on TV. A few days later Jerry was shoehorned into a movie called *Jamboree* in which he sang his next big hit, "Great Balls of Fire." Writer Ben Grevatt described one of Jerry's performances in his "On the Beat" newspaper column:

> Jerry Lee Lewis with the craziest vest you ever saw (trimmed with leopard skin) and combing his hair frantically between numbers, was particularly rough on the piano. We've long expected to see a piano crack up under his special kind of pounding. Sure enough, the tired looking instrument couldn't take it. Interrupting his act, Lewis informed the audience: "Well, man, I guess this piano's had it," while assistants rushed on stage to try to repair the damaged strings.

"Breathless" was on its way up the charts as Lewis began a concert tour in England. Then word got out that the thirteen-year-old lady with him was his wife . . . his cousin, yet. Lewis was booed off the stage, and promoter J. Arthur Rank quickly replaced him. At the airport back in the States a swarm of reporters eagerly awaited his arrival.

"Tell us about this reception in London," one reporter asked, barely able to conceal his delight. Jerry remained calm, with wife Myra Gale Brown at his side, and politely replied, "We had a very good reception, Sir." Of course the reporter knew the truth—the story had been in all of the newspapers—but he continued to bait Lewis nevertheless. When the singer didn't bite he turned to Myra, who was innocently chewing her gum, and started in on her. But Myra confirmed her husband's story. Finally, unable to restrain himself, the reporter asked when they were married. "Well," Lewis replied, "we leave our personal questions out of this, Sir."

Actually, Jerry Lee Lewis had been married twice before. In 1950 he married Dorothy Barton, a preacher's daughter. Possibly to impress her father, Lewis once stood in the pulpit himself, dishing out the gospel according to The Killer, like a page right out of *Elmer Gantry*. Jerry's second marriage in 1953 was to Jane Mitcham, who bore him two children. But it was his marriage to Myra that all but finished him. Once the word was out, disc jockeys refused to play his records, and after *High School Confidential* he wasn't seen in another movie for twenty years. He began playing county fairs and sleazy bars, yet the experience didn't seem to humble him. "If you don't like what I'm doing you can kiss my ass!" he would bark at what he considered an unappreciative audience. For over a decade his life was riddled with unpleasant events. His son, Steve Allen Lewis, drowned in a swimming pool. Myra divorced him after thirteen years of being beaten and cuffed into submission. His fourth wife left him after only two weeks. Jerry shot his bass player accidentally with a .357 Magnum. His fifth wife died under mysterious circumstances. Timothy White in *Rock Stars* recounts that Elvis Presley wasn't anxious to see ol' Jerry when he showed up at his place one night, all tanked up and hot under the collar, yelling and ranting, brandishing a .38 derringer. "I wanna see Elvis!" he screamed at the guard at the front gate. "You just tell him the Killer's here! Git on that damn house phone and call him! Who the hell does that sonofabitch think he is? Doesn't wanna be disturbed. He ain't no damn better'n anybody else!" The Killer was escorted not to Presley's front door but to the local hoosegow. He was pulled off a stage in Baton Rouge by cousin Jimmy Swaggart, who took him home to dry him out. Swaggart went through Jerry's place like a white tornado, emptying bottles of booze and pills into toilets and sinks. Jerry later remarked that Swaggart saved his life.

Recently, after nearly a decade of effort by producer Adam Fields, a movie was made about the Killer's years with Myra, based on her book (co-authored by Murray Silver) titled *Great Balls of Fire!* And the Killer seems to be on top again. Yet his performances are far from consistent. Producer Fields decided to make his movie when he saw him in an impressive performance at the Palomino in North Hollywood. Others report the Killer walked through the performance they saw. One account has him playing "Over the Rainbow" for a full thirty minutes before he was dragged off of the stage to the accompaniment of a jeering, disappointed crowd. Great balls of fire, indeed.

The Music

Jerry Lee Lewis: "High School Confidential," available on Sun records.

NOTE: MGM also released a single: "Christopher Columbus Digs the Jive" and "High School Drag."

The Reception

"Good acting, skillful direction . . . and the excellent film editing . . . give this film a technical proficiency beyond that found in most low-budget quickies devoted to the same subject matter . . . Jerry Lee Lewis sings a rock 'n' roll theme song . . . which wrenches the ears. . . ." — *The Hollywood Reporter.*

"We did way above average on this picture on a mid-week. Of course, most of the crowd was made up of teenagers and younger children." — Charles E. Smith, an Illinois exhibitor.

". . . the film's crowning absurdity is its official-sounding homily on the evils of high school drug-taking, delivered over a final carefree sequence showing Tony's alcoholic, nymphomaniac Aunt Gwen necking in the back seat of a car, while Tony sits in front with two blondes — one a schoolgirl described as having recently abandoned 'the weed' for 'ordinary' cigarettes; the other a progressive school-mistress." — *Monthly Film Bulletin.*

"This is a real good picture of its type. The business was much better and we were very glad, of course. The story was good and is true." — Harry Hawkinson, Minnesota exhibitor.

"Although the presentation seems to exploit to the fullest every facet of this evil situation, it does so skillfully and with compelling effect." — *Variety.*

"Above average business to a crowd pleaser. . . . Shows what could happen to your school or to your kids. Seemed to have approval of few parents we saw."—Ben Spainhouer, Kansas exhibitor.

". . . the best teen-age drama since *Blackboard Jungle*."—*Dig.*

"Very good picture about marijuana and teenagers. . . . One of the best Wednesday night crowds I've had in a long time."—James Hardy, Indiana exhibitor.

"Russ Tamblyn and Mamie Van Doren make a hit with the teenagers. This one is very good; some action, some rock and roll, and a good story. Above average business."—L.C. Brazil, an Arkansas exhibitor.

The Cast

Russ Tamblyn (Tony Baker/Mike Wilson), Jan Sterling (Arlene Williams), John Drew Barrymore (J.I. Coleridge), Mamie Van Doren (Gwen Dulaine), Diane Jergens (Joan Staples), Jerry Lee Lewis (himself), Ray Anthony (Box), Jackie Coogan (Mr. A), Charles Chaplin, Jr. (Quinn), Burt Douglas (Jukey Judlow), Jody Fair (Doris), Phillipa Fallon (poetess), Robin Raymond (Kitty), James Todd (Jack Staples), Lyle Talbot (William Remington Kane; narrator), William Wellman, Jr. (Wheeler-Dealer), Texas Joe Foster (henchman), Diana Darrin (Gloria), Carl Thayler (Petey), Irwin Berke (Morino), Michael Landon.

The Credits

Director Jack Arnold, *Producer* Albert Zugsmith, *Screenplay* Lewis Meltzer and Robert Blees from a story by Robert Blees, *Director of Photography* Harold J. Marzorati, *Art Directors* William A. Horning and Hans Peters, *Sound* Dr. Wesley C. Miller, *Editor* Ben Lewis. B&W Scope 85 min. MGM.

Sources

Boxoffice, Vol. 71, No. 6, July 1, 1957, pg. 24; Vol. 73, No. 6, June 2, 1958, pg. 8; Vol. 74, No. 4, November 17, 1958, pg. 10; Vol. 74, No. 10, December 29, 1958, pg. 10; Vol. 74, No. 13, January 19, 1959, pg. 10; Vol. 74, No. 23, March 30, 1959, pg. 10; Vol. 75, No. 5, May 25, 1959, pg. 18; Escott, "Jerry Lee Lewis, The Ferriday Wild Man"; McCarthy and Flynn, *Kings of the Bs;* White, *Rock Stars.*

Ad for *Hot Rod Gang.*

Hot Rod Gang (1958)

Known in England as *Fury Unleashed* and shot under the title *Hot Rod Rock,* this was a pretty square film under any title. It was written by American International's resident writer Lou Rusoff, the brother-in-law of AIP's vice president, Sam Arkoff. Rusoff was later responsible for the first *Beach Party* movie, which kicked off a series that starred Frankie Avalon and Annette Funicello. "He wrote, constructively, some very good screenplays," claimed the musical director for *Hot Rod Gang,* Ronald Stein. Stein had to admit, however, when it came to writing dialog for teenagers, Rusoff was out of his element.

John Ashley, usually the villain of AIP's teenpix, was the hero of this piece. As John Abernathy the Third, Ashley is forced to live a double life to inherit the family fortune. In the presence of his two maiden aunts he dresses in suits and plays classical music on his violin. Away from home he sings rock and roll music and races hot rods. When one of his buddies needs cash to build a car to enter in a national competition, Ashley disguises himself with a beard so he can sing professionally to raise the money. He's eventually found out by his two aunts who surprise him by supporting his efforts and expressing a liking for the music he plays.

In an earlier AIP film, *Dragstrip Girl,* Ashley and Frank Gorshin sang a few lines from a song called "Dragstrip Baby," which was apparently a preamble to his appearance in this film. "I did what I thought at the time was a dynamite impersonation of Presley," Ashley recalled with a smirk. "Elvis and I laughed about it later."

Ashley belts out three songs in the film, including an upbeat

Top: John Ashley (right) is rehearsing "Hit and Run Lover." Bottom: (Left–right) Gene Vincent, Jody Fair and John Ashley. From *Hot Rod Gang*.

**Left: (Left–right) Wee Willie Williams, Gene Vincent, and Be-Bop Harrell.
Right: Record jacket from *Hot Rod Gang*.**

version of "Annie Laurie," "an old Scottish song originally recorded in
1910 by John McCormack. But Ashley's efforts, energetic though they
may have been, were overshadowed by Gene Vincent and the Blue
Caps. Like Ashley, Vincent was one of the many singers heavily influenced by Elvis Presley. He was, in fact, signed by Capitol Records
during the company's search for an Elvis soundalike. The song that did
the trick was "Be-Bop-a-Lula," which became Vincent's first and only
gold record, supposedly inspired by a comic book. "Me and Don Graves
were looking at this bloody comic book," Vincent told a reporter years
later. "It was called *Little Lulu* and I said: 'Hell, man, it's bebopaLulu.'
And he said: 'Yeah, man, swinging.' And we wrote the song. Just like
that. And some man came to hear it and he bought the song for $25.
Right. Twenty-five dollars! And I recorded it and told all my friends that
I was going to get a Cadillac, because all rock 'n' roll singers had
Cadillacs," from *The Encyclopedia of Pop Rock & Soul.*
      Depending on who's doing the telling, Vincent wrote the song on
the way to California from Virginia, in his car or on a train. Or he mailed
a demo record to Capitol.

Equally vague are the circumstances surrounding Vincent's leg injury. While he was stationed in Korea during his tour of duty with the navy he stepped on a mine. Or was shot. He was discharged and sent home to recuperate, with or without his leg. Or he injured it in a motorcycle accident. It was the pain, supposedly, that caused him to drink heavily.

"I thought he was totally mad when he'd had some drink," said Little Richard, who toured with Vincent in Australia in 1957. Richard recalled an evening when Vincent tried to push him out of a speeding car, from *Life & Times of Little Richard* by Charles White.

Born Vincent Eugene Craddock on February 11, 1935, he learned to play the guitar in his teens and after his discharge from the navy began performing on live country music radio shows in Norfolk. He formed the Blue Caps (named after the hat President Dwight Eisenhower always wore on the golf course): "Jumpin'" Jack Neal, "Be-Bop" Dickie Harrell, "Galloping" Cliff Gallup, and "Wee" Willie Williams. They had a mild and brief career in America, after which Vincent moved to England, where fans were more enthusiastic about his brand of singing. But his drinking caught up with him, and in 1971 he died from a perforated ulcer. He often bragged that he'd spent more money than most people ever earned and was proud of the fact that on Hollywood and Vine, just outside of the Hollywood Palace, a star bore his name.

The Music

John Ashley: "Annie Laurie," "Believe Me," and "Hit and Run Lover."

Gene Vincent and the Blue Caps: "Baby Blue," "Dance in the Street," and "Dancin' to the Bop" (performed off stage), released on a Capitol EP with an additional song, "Lovely Loretta." All of the songs are still available.

The Reception

"If narrative rambles afield at times, pic more than makes up for it in youthful action. . . . Film is given an r-r shot by Gene Vincent and his Red Caps [sic] . . . John Ashley makes a good impression as the lead, handily warbling a couple of songs. . . ."—*Variety*.

"Swallow your pride and play this and *High School Hellcats*. You won't gain any prestige, but you can't bank that." — Jim Fraser, an exhibitor in Minnesota.

"The youthful spectators, when I was present, greeted Ashley's tortured and orgiastic attempts to do an Elvis Presley with hoots of ridicule." — *The Hollywood Reporter*.

"Same as all the rest — GOOD." — Harold Bell, an exhibitor in Quebec.

"Yet another essay on the old teen-age theme of the 'sins of the squares,' though with some claim to being the tritest entrant in the field to date. The comedy misfires woefully, the performances are overstated to the point of caricature, and the general level is decidedly moronic." — *Monthly Film Bulletin*.

"I played this as a combo with *High School Hellcats* to good Monday and Tuesday business." — Simon Cherivtch, an exhibitor in New Jersey.

The Cast

John Ashley (John Abernathy the Third), Jody Fair (Lois Cavendish), Gene Vincent (himself), Steve Drexel (Mark), Henry McCann (Dave), Maureen Arthur (Marley), Gloria Grant (Tammy), Dorothy Newman (Anastasia Abernathy), Helen Spring (Abigail Abernathy), Lister Dorr (Dryden Philpot), Doodles Weaver (Wesley Cavendish), Russ Bender (Bill), Claire Dubray (Agatha), Dub Taylor (Al Berrywhiff), Scott Peters (Jack), Robert Whiteside (Jimmy), Simmy Bow (Johnny Red Eye), Earl McDaniels (himself), Kay Wheeler (specialty dancer).

The Credits

Director Lew Landers, *Producer-Screenplay* Lou Rusoff, *Executive Producer* Charles "Buddy" Rogers, *Assistant Director* Austen Jewell, *Director of Photography* Floyd Crosby, A.S.C., *Editor* Robert S. Eisen, *Art Director* Don Ament, *Sound* Anthony Carras, *Set* Harry Reif, *Music* Ronald Stein, ASCAP. A James H. Nicholson and Samuel Z. Arkoff Production. B&W 72 min. American International Picture.

Sources

Boxoffice, Vol. 74, No. 8, December 15, 1958, pg. 18; Vol. 74, No. 20, March 9, 1959, pg. 10; Vol. 75, No. 20, September 7, 1959, pg. 10;

Herman, *Rock 'n' Roll Babylon;* Larson, "Film Music of Ronald Stein";
Stambler, *Encyclopedia of Pop Rock and Soul;* White, *Life and Times of
Little Richard.*

How to Make a Monster (1958)

How to Make was not really a teenage movie, much less a rock and
roll movie. It was what producer Herman Cohen's *I Was a Teenage
Werewolf* would have been like if he'd focused on the crazed doctor instead of the young man he was corrupting. Still, this was aimed at the
eighteen and under crowd and for that reason contained a rock and roll
number performed by actor John Ashley, who took a brief shot at a singing career.

Born December 25, 1934, in Kansas City, Ashley was the adopted
son of Roger and Lucille Atchley. Today Ashley tries to be nonchalant
about his various endeavors, whether singing, acting or producing. He
describes his induction into American International in much the same
way one might describe being drafted into the military. Supposedly, he
was waiting for his girlfriend to audition for a role (which she didn't get)
when he was spotted by AIP's resident writer Lou Rusoff, who thought
he was perfect for the villain of his *Dragstrip Girl.* Until that moment
Ashley never even thought about being an actor. AIP signed him to a
three-picture contract, which ultimately led to a riff between Ashley
and AIP's vice president, Sam Arkoff. Ashley was offered a dramatic part
on TV's "Matinee Theatre" opposite Janis Paige. AIP wanted Ashley to
star in *Hot Rod Gang.* Ashley asked for a postponement so he could do
the TV show, which he felt might pull him out of the B-movies. Arkoff
wouldn't budge. Ashley angrily left AIP with every intention of doing
the TV show regardless of his contract, and Arkoff enjoined him from
doing the show. "I never really forgave Sam for that," Ashley remarked.
"He could have let me do that show and still had me in his movie."

Ashley dropped away from AIP for a little while after this picture,
though he was back in the *Beach Party* series that ran through the mid-
sixties. At the end of the decade he alternately produced films for AIP
(and his own company), in which he usually appeared. He has since
stopped acting, which he says he doesn't miss, and has produced several
successful TV series. "Even as a little boy I loved movies, but acting was
something I fell into."

John Ashley in an all-stops-out production number in which he sings "You Gotta Have Ee-ooo." From *How to Make a Monster.*

The Music

John Ashley: "You've Got to Have Ee-ooo."

The Reception

". . . is rather mild as these exploitation pictures go. . . . The script has some sharp dialog and occasionally pungent Hollywood Talk ("That's the way the footage cuts") although these aspects will be largely lost on the audiences this picture will attract."—*Variety.*

". . . has a rather good song, 'You've Got to Have Ee---OOO,' a joint effort of Paul Dunlap and Skip Redwine. . . ."—*Hollywood Citizens News.*

". . . better than its jivey title might indicate."—*Mirror News.*

"It is not a do-it-yourself treatise on how to fashion your own household eyesores. Rather, it's a torpid tale without even the so-called horror which is supposed to attract adolescents."—*The Los Angeles Examiner.*

"The massed small fry in the audience expressed its preference, but a sort of scattered acclamation, for real monsters rather than madeup ones."—*Hollywood Reporter.*

The Cast

Robert H. Harris (Pete Drummond), Paul Brinegar (Rivero), Gary Conway (Tony Mantell), Gary Clarke (Larry Drake), Malcolm Atterbury (Richards), Dennis Cross (Monahan), Morris Ankrum (Captain Hancock), Walter Reed (Detective Thompson), Paul Maxwell (Jeff Clayton), Eddie Marr (John Nixon), Heather Ames (Arlene Dow), Robert Shayne (Gary Droz), Rod Dana (lab technician), Jacqueline Ebeier (Jane), Joan Chandler (Marilyn), Thomas B. Henry (Martin Brace), John Phillips (Detective Jones), Pauline Myers (Millie), John Ashley (himself).

The Credits

Director Herbert L. Strock, *Producer* Herman Cohen, *Executive Producers* James H. Nicholson and Samuel Z. Arkoff, *Story & Screenplay* Kenneth Langtry and Herman Cohen, *Director of Photography* Maury Gertzman, A.S.C., *Production Manager* Herb Mendelson, *Makeup* Philip Scheer and Paul Blaisdell, *Art Director* Leslie Thomas, *Assistant Director* Herb Mendelson, *Set* Morris Hoffman, *Sound* Herman Lewis, *Music* Paul Dunlap. B&W (color sequence) 75 min. A Sunset Production. American International Picture.

Sources

Lamparski, *Whatever Became of. . .?* Vol. 10.

Jailhouse Rock (1957)

This was the third film to feature Elvis Presley, another version of Presley's own rise to fame. Unlike *Loving You*, which was a gussied-up account in sparkling VistaVision and color, this one is black and white and close to film noir. Presley's not confused and frightened like he was in the previous film; he's vicious and greedy.

Jailed for manslaughter, Presley, as Vince Everett, learns to play guitar in prison from a hillbilly singer named Hunk Houghton. Released, Presley embarks on a singing career, and by the time Houghton shows up to take advantage of a contract he signed Everett to when they were cellmates, Everett is riding a wave of success. And he's become a first-class butt. Houghton becomes one of his flunkies until he gets fed up and socks Everett in the throat. It looks for a while as if Everett will never sing again, but an operation does the trick, and Everett's been humbled in the process.

The title was changed to *Jailhouse Kid* on April 27 and changed back again before the picture had its world premiere at Loew's State Theatre in Memphis. The title song became a double-sided hit with another song from the film, "Treat Me Nice." The *Jailhouse Rock* number was choreographed by Presley and is probably the most imaginatively staged number of his entire film output. In the film Elvis is backed by a be-bop style chorus which was dispensed with on the hit single. The film version is now available, as is almost anything with Presley in it.

The title song and three others from the film were penned by Jerry Leiber and Mike Stoller, the hottest team of the fifties. Leiber (born in Baltimore on April 25, 1933) and Stoller (born March 13, 1933, in New York) created dozens of hits for Presley, the Coasters, the Drifters, Procol Harum, Stealer's Wheel . . . the list goes on. And they're still at it. "Jailhouse Rock" was written on spec, as were all of the songs for the film. Because Presley's name on a song was as good as gold, writers were expected to work for free in the hope their song would be chosen and generally had to give up more of their rights than would have normally been expected. But with Presley's track record he (or rather Tom Parker) could call the shots.

Two weeks after the movie was completed, female lead Judy Tyler was killed in a head-on auto collision. Funeral services were held on July 24, 1957, at the Frank E. Campbell Church.

The Music

Elvis Presley: "Jailhouse Rock," "Treat Me Nice," "Young and Beautiful," "I Want to Be Free," "Don't Leave Me Now," and "(You're So Square), Baby I Don't Care," available on RCA. The first two songs

Ad for *Jailhouse Rock.*

were issued as a single. All songs but "Treat Me Nice" were issued as an EP.

The Reception

"Film is packed with the type of material Presley's followers go for and it's a cinch a considerable portion of the populace, particularly the cats, will find this . . . right down their alley."—*Variety.*

"No use pushing this for it pushes itself. . . . The youngsters like to brag how many times they've seen it. Their enthusiasm is so contagious that the oldsters have to admit it has something special. . . ."—Velva Otts, a Texas exhibitor.

"Much of what was considered objectional in the delivery of his songs has been minimized. The result is an entertaining film with some enjoyable musical numbers in the still popular rock and roll vein."—*Motion Picture Exhibitor.*

"I thought Elvis Presley had lost a little of his popularity but *Jailhouse Rock* did the best business of his three pictures."—S.T. Jackson, an Alabama exhibitor.

"The problem with making a picture with a personality whose appeal has always been to one group is that of broadening the appeal without losing the loyal segment you started with. . . . [This picture] may well be the most successful attempt."—*The Hollywood Reporter.*

"The adverse publicity one of the South African bearded (for obvious reasons) critics gave this one did every exhibitor's heart good, and filled the house. . . . The critic said of it that it was like the writing on a toilet wall. The papers here for weeks were full of contempt and fury at his remarks, and all this helped at the box-office."—Dave S. Klein, an exhibitor in Northern Rhodesia.

"Presley sings six songs and has a particularly obnoxious, overtly obscene style. We are informed that to many, listening to these songs and watching Presley's gyrations will more than compensate for the annoyance of sitting through a distasteful story, ugly in its telling, performance, and presentation."—*Cue.* (But how did they like it?)

"I now have the answer to the question, how to keep the theatres open. Just get ten more like Elvis Presley. With rain, high waters, flu and every other kind of thing to put the hex on business, it still did way above average. . . . It's just amazing how everyone goes for Presley, even the small kids below school age. And the colored people came in large numbers."—Victor Weber, an Arkansas exhibitor.

"For movie-goers who may not care for that personality, Presley himself offers in the film a word of consolation: "Don't worry," he says, "I'll grow on

Elvis rocks at the jailhouse.

In *Jailhouse Rock*, Elvis is seen on the giving (top) and receiving (bottom) end of a punch.

Elvis is cornered in *Jailhouse Rock*.

you." If he does it will be quite a depressing job to scrape him off." —
Time.

"Very good picture. Presley good in this, but the B rating hurts and
not too big here, as the kids saw it elsewhere. Sunday business equalled
the three-day run on *Bernardine*, so TV overexposure evidently hurts
Boone." — Ken Christianson, a North Dakota exhibitor.

"If Presley's earlier opuses pleased you, there shouldn't be anything
in this one to offend; if you have an ear for anything except Presley,
however, you aren't likely to find anything here that will revise your
opinion." — *New York Herald Tribune*.

"I, personally, am not stuck on Mr. Elvis, but who am I to judge.
I had all the students from the towns around. I never saw so many kids
and students in any one show in this theatre before, but they were very
well behaved." — F.L. Murray, a Saskatchewan exhibitor.

"He sings well, but is not yet an actor." — *Teen*.

"For fans of the star this may be enough, but as a piece of story-
telling the picture is distinctly flat. The title number, very much over-
staged, has a certain primitive verve." — *Monthly Film Bulletin*.

The Cast

Elvis Presley (Vince Everett), Judy Tyler (Peggy Van Alden), Mickey Shaughnessy (Hunk Houghton), Vaughn Taylor (Mr. Shores), Jennifer Holden (Sherry Wilson), Dean Jones (Teddy Talbot), Anne Neyland (Laury Jackson).

The Credits

Director Richard Thorpe, *Producer* Pandro S. Berman, *Associate Producer* Kathryn Hereford, *Screenplay* Guy Trosper based on a story by Ned Young, *Director of Photography* Robert Bronner, A.S.C., *Art Directors* William A. Horning and Randall Duell, *Assistant Director* Robert E. Relyea, *Editor* Ralph E. Winters, A.C.E. B&W/Scope 96 min. Avon Productions. Metro-Goldwyn-Mayer.

Sources

Boxoffice, Vol. 74, No. 4, November 17, 1958, pg. 10; Vol. 74, No. 9, December 21, 1957, pg. 13; Vol. 72, No. 11, January 6, 1958, pg. 11; Vol. 73, No. 21, September 15, 1958, pg. 4; Carr and Farren, *Elvis*.

Jamboree (1957)

Like the previous rock movie from producers Max J. Rosenberg and Milton Subotsky *(Rock, Rock, Rock)*, *Jamboree* was as close to wall to wall music as any film would get until the next decade when *The T.A.M.I. Show* (1964) dispensed with plot altogether.

"*Jamboree* was a studio picture," said Rosenberg. "We had quote a plot unquote and we had recognizable actors. It was shot on the old Fox studio at Tenth Avenue and 56th Street. It was probably a three-week shoot."

The quote plot unquote concerned a pair of singers who fall in love during an audition. Their romance is under constant threat from the demands and pressures of the music business. Their trials and tribulations are played out between recording sessions, and true love triumphs during the final record hop.

Warner Bros. had handled the foreign rights to Rosenberg's and Subotsky's *Rock, Rock, Rock,* but the Distributor's Corporation of

Ad for *Jamboree* shows original title of *Disc Jockey Jamboree*.

America (DCA) handled domestic. When Warner Bros. saw the potential for profit they decided to bankroll a rock movie of their own.

There are almost as many disc jockeys in the film as there are songs, a clever gimmick since each DJ was certain to plug the film on his show. In addition to Dick Clark, whose face wasn't quite as familiar then as it would soon become, there's Joe Smith (WVDA, Boston), Joe Finan (KWY, Cleveland), Keith Sandy (CKEY, Toronto), Zenas Sears (WAOK, Atlanta), Barry Kaye (WJAS, Pittsburgh), Sandy Singer (WTCN, Minneapolis), Ray Perkins (KIMN, Denver), Gerry Myers (CKOY, Ottawa), Jocko Henderson (WOV, New York), Ed Bonner (KXOK, St. Louis), Robin Seymour (WKMH, Detroit), Dick Whittinghill (KMPC, Hollywood—often seen on Jack Webb's "Dragnet" TV show), Howard Miller (WIND, Chicago), Werner Goetze (Bayerische Rundfunk, Munch), Chris Howland (West Deutsche Rundfunk, Cologne), Jack Payne (BBC, London), and Jack Jackson (ATV, London).

The Music

Most of the performers featured in this film had hit records but with few exceptions opted to sing a new song in the hope of making a new hit. One of the exceptions was Jerry Lee Lewis, who was a last-minute addition to the roster. His appearance on Steve Allen's Sunday night TV program had propelled Lewis into an overnight success (to use a meaningless phrase). He was signed for this picture the following

Top: Buddy Knox (center) and band. Bottom: Carl Perkins and band. From *Jamboree.*

month, and in it he sang "Great Balls of Fire," a song given to Lewis by the movie's musical director, Otis Blackwell.

Carl Perkins sings "Glad All Over." His biggest hit was "Blue Suede Shoes," which he sang on Perry Como's TV show, a segment included in Columbia's video tape production *Rock and Roll: The Early Years.* He claimed it was the easiest song he ever wrote. The idea came from the kids by the bandstand in Jackson, Tennessee, where Perkins lived in a government project with his wife, Velda. The kids were so proud of their new city shoes it inspired the song. "You gotta be real poor to care about new shoes like I did," Perkins remarked. He sent a tape to Sam Phillips at Sun Records. Phillips was looking for a replacement for Elvis Presley, who'd left Sun for a better deal at RCA Victor. It's doubtful Perkins would have ever been much of a threat to Presley (who also recorded "Blue Suede Shoes"). He didn't have the looks or the charisma. Born in Tiptonville, Tennessee, on April 9, 1932, Perkins had a major career setback in 1956 when a near-fatal car accident outside Wilmington, Delaware, kept him bedridden for the better part of a year. Bitter, he took to drink and had decided to give up show business when Johnny Cash asked him to join him for a two-day concert. "We got there and John had me come up and do a couple of songs. That two-day tour lasted ten years." Eventually Perkins left Cash and formed his own band. Around 1986 he let people know he was interested in doing a TV special. George Harrison, Dave Edmunds, Ringo Starr and the Stray Cats signed on. Perkins said doing the show was the highlight of his career. "To be up there playin' with those guys, really workin', seein' the sweat drip down their noses, made me feel highly honored."

Jimmy Bowen and Buddy Knox sing "Cross Over" and "Hula Love," respectively. Both singers hailed from Texas. Knox was born there (July 20, 1933), and Bowen's family moved to Dumas when Jimmy was eight. They co-authored Knox's biggest hit, "Party Doll," written around the same time Knox cooked up "Hula Love," inspired by Metropolitan Opera Quartet's "My Hula Hula love." Bowen's biggest hit was "I'm Sticking with You," another Knox-Bowen composition, recorded during the "Party Doll" session. He became the head Fred at Electra/Asylum's Nashville division. Knox continues to tour and lives on a farm outside of Winnipeg, Manitoba, Canada.

Making his film debut in *Jamboree* is Frankie Avalon, accompanied by Rocco and His Saints. Born Francis Thomas Avallone, he was set (legend has it) to be a boxer until he saw Kirk Douglas in *Young Man*

Record jacket for *Jamboree* soundtrack.

with a Horn. "It inspired me so much," recalled the singer, "I asked my father if I could get a trumpet. He was elated, being a frustrated musician himself." Papa picked one up in a pawn shop for $15, and before long Avalon was playing professionally on a regular TV show. When childhood friend Bob Marcucci got into the record business he wanted Avalon on his label, but as a singer. Avalon was with Rocco and His Saints at the time, so Marcucci signed the lot and got them the audition for *Jamboree*, then called *Disc Jockey Jamboree*. Their song "Cupid" didn't go anywhere but their next one, "Dede Dinah," hit the top ten. Avalon's biggest success was "Venus," the third best-selling record of 1959, right under "Mack the Knife" and "The Battle of New Orleans"—to give you an idea of the music scene that year. Avalon turned his attention to acting and is best remembered for the *Beach Party* series, affectionately recalled in a film spearheaded by Avalon and his co-star Annette Funicello called *Back to the Beach*, in which the two stars poke fun at the series and themselves.

Frankie Avalon with Rocco and His Saints: "Teacher's Pet," available on Chancellor.

Jimmy Bowen: "Cross Over," available on Roulette.

Paul Carr: "If Not for You," "Twenty-Four Hours a Day" and "Who Are We to Say," the latter two with Connie Francis, available on Warner Bros. soundtrack album.

Count Basie and Orchestra: "Jamboree" and "One O'Clock Jump."

Ron Colby: "Toreador."

Fats Domino: "Wait and See," available on Imperial.

The Four Coins: "A Broken Promise."

Connie Francis: "For Children of All Ages" and "Siempre."

Charlie Gracie: "Cool Baby."

Martha Lou Harp: "Crazy to Care."

Jerry Lee Lewis: "Great Balls of Fire," available on Sun.

Buddy Knox: "Hula Love," available on Roulette.

Lewis Lymon and the Teenchords: "Gone."

Andy Martin: "Record Hop Tonight."

Carl Perkins: "Glad All Over," released on Sun.

Joe Williams: "I Don't Like You No More."

Slim Whitman: "Unchained My Heart," available on Imperial.

NOTE: All songs were part of a Warner Bros. soundtrack album.

The Reception

". . . was filmed with a single objective — to present a parade of stand-up singing talent. Film is dated in concept, reminiscent of the early days of musical films when producers slapped a group of singing acts together, but it's okay for . . . the jukebox trade." — *Variety*.

"People insisted it was filmed largely from a TV show they had seen — same background and all. Still, all in all, okay for this sort." — Penny Harris, a Texas exhibitor.

"Although merit seems to have little to do with the success or failure of these films, it should be noted that *Jamboree* is superior to the general run of such pictures." — *Hollywood Reporter*.

"Seems lately that these rock and roll shows have to be just so wild or they don't go. As for myself, I enjoyed it except for the two who played the leading roles. They could have stayed home." — Harold Bell, a Quebec exhibitor.

"We thought most of the rock and roll numbers were funny and that most of the performers doing these numbers were selected deliberately because of their youth. In one way or the other they were reminiscent of Elvis Presley which is probably also intentional. Jerry Lee Lewis is particularly amusing as he stares mindlessly tinkering at a piano and periodically lets out a yelp of anguish." — *Hollywood Citizens News.*

"While the story is hardly original, it has the advantage of some good natural dialog and some fine performances which most other films in this genre have lacked." — *Motion Picture Herald.*

"Youngsters who enjoy this brand of music should get their fill as one rock and roll number follows another with amazing rapidity. There is some attempt at a story along the way but it hasn't a chance against the noise furnished by the so-called musical guest stars." — *Motion Picture Exhibitor.*

". . . the singers are as undistinguished as the plot. Exceptions include Joe Williams and Fats Domino — genuine blues singers worthy of better company — and Count Basie's immaculate band." — *Monthly Film Bulletin.*

The Cast

Kay Medford (Grace Shaw), Robert Pastine (Lew Arthur), Freda Halloway (Honey Wynn), Paul Carr (Pete Porter), Fats Domino, Buddy Knox, Charlie Gracie, Count Basie and His Orchestra, Jodie Sands, Slim Whitman, Ron Coby, Andy Martin, Jerry Lee Lewis, Jimmy Bowen, The Four Coins, Joe Williams, Carl Perkins, Lewis Lymon and the Teenchords, Connie Francis (singing voice of Freda Halloway), Rocco and His Saints, Frankie Avalon, Joe Smith, Joe Finan, Keith Sandy, Zenas Sears, Milt Grant, Dick Clark, Barry Kaye, Sandy Singer, Ray Perkins, Gerry Myers, Jocko Henderson, Ed Bonner, Robin Seymour, Dick Whittinghill, Howard Miller, Werner Goetze, Chris Howland, Jack Payne, and Jack Jackson.

The Credits

Director Roy Lockwood, *Producer* Max J. Rosenberg and Milton Subotsky, *Screenplay* Leonard Kantor, *Director of Photography* Jack Etra, *Art Director* Paul Barnes, *Editor* Robert Broekman, *Associate Producer* Herman Klappert, *Music* Otis Blackwell.

Sources

Boxoffice, Vol. 72, No. 25, April 14, 1958, pg. 14; Vol. 73, No. 7, June 9, 1958, pg. 6; Escott, "Jerry Lee Lewis, the Ferriday Wild Man"; Nite, *Rock On*; Stambler, *Encyclopedia of Pop Rock and Soul*.

Juke Box Rhythm (1959)

For the most part *Juke* steered away from rock and roll in keeping with the trend begun when the Payola scandal began (see *Because They're Young*). The film was unavailable for viewing, ergo the following information is pieced together from two trade reviews which in all probability rehashed studio press releases, notorious for mistakes often passed on by reviewers in the hope of circumventing the process of actually seeing the movie.

A young singer tries to persuade a European princess to buy her coronation wardrobe from a junkman who aspires to be a designer. The commission is enough to finance a Broadway show produced by the singer's father, avoiding the need for dad to borrow from a sexually sophisticated and wealthy lady. Dad shouldn't have too much fun.

The Music

Johnny Otis does the song he became known for, "Willie and the Hand Jive," the theme for his television show in the late fifties. Otis grew up in California, born December 28, 1921. He wasn't interested in music until after high school, when he saw Count Basie at the San Francisco World's Fair. Otis taught himself to play drums and played with a lot of bands before he formed his own, which he called the Johnny Otis Rhythm and Blues Caravan. Savoy Records heard about them, and they cut a few discs for the company. By 1950 he was on a roll in the rhythm and blues business. Otis kept his show on the road constantly. Five years later he gave it up to be home with his children and became a disc jockey. But he'd keep his hand in now and then by playing some of the concerts his station promoted. In 1957 he cut a record for Capitol, a song written by Otis and his partner Hal Zeiger. It bombed in the United States but did okay in England, so Zeiger went to England to see what was going on. He came back with the news of the skiffle craze. He told Otis there was no dancing, so the kids did a thing called the hand jive. He thought Otis should write a song about it. Otis' career went through a rough period in the sixties but the singer was back at it again in the seventies. He later joined the ministry and dropped out of the music business again but continues to resurface from time to time.

Earl Grant Trio: "I Feel It Right Here" and "Last Night."

George Jessel: "Spring Is the Time for Remembering."

Jack Jones: "The Freeze" and "Make Room for Joy."

Jo Morrow: "Let's Fall in Love."

Johnnie Otis: "Willie and the Hand Jive," available on Capitol.

The Treniers: "Get Out of the Car."

The Reception

"Sam Katzman continues his parade of pleasant little musicals . . . contrived but acceptable. . . ." — *Variety*.

"This picture smells — but so did 90 per cent of the other rock 'n' roll pictures. Unlike the others, though, this one did no business at all. Have the kids finally gotten their fill of this trash? I hope the ones here have." — L.R. DuBose, an exhibitor in Texas.

"This is a nicely integrated program musical aimed primarily at the teenage market, although older patrons have not been entirely neglected." — *Motion Picture Herald*.

". . . brims with music and overflows with energy. . . ." — *Film Daily*.

". . . teenagers should come out in droves. . . ." — *Boxoffice*.

The Cast

Jo Morrow (princess), Jack Jones (singer), Brian Donlevy (Broadway producer), George Jessel (himself), Hans Conried (designer/garbage man), Karin Booth (wealthy man-chaser), Marjorie Reynolds (Donlevy's devoted wife), Frieda Inescort (the royal chaperone), Edgar Barrier (ambassador), Fritz Feld, Hortense Petra.

The Credits

Director Arthur Dreifuss, *Producer* Sam Katzman, *Screenplay* Mary P. McCall and Earl Baldwin, *Story* Lou Morheim, *Director of Photography* Fred Jackman, *Art Director* Paul Palmentola, *Choreographer*

Hal Belfer, *Sound* John Livadary, Josh Westmoreland, *Editor* Saul A. Goodkind. B&W 83 min. A Clover Production. A Columbia Picture.

Sources

Boxoffice, Vol. 75, No. 21, September 14, 1959, pg. 10; Stambler, *Encyclopedia of Pop Rock and Soul.*

King Creole (1958)

Elvis Presley's fourth film was the second for producer Hal Wallis, who hereafter would take the singer away from his tough guy persona and turn him into a lightweight Howard Keel. Presley's subsequent induction into the army would have a drastic effect on his screen image and his choice of music. Between themselves, Uncle Sam and Tom Parker managed to amputate the rock from Presley's roll. *King Creole* marked the last film appearance of Presley before the fire went out.

Presley plays Danny Fisher, an angry kid growing up in the French Quarter of New Orleans. Tired of being poor and watching his father kowtow to his unsympathetic boss, Danny quits school and falls in with a street gang. He quits the gang after he finds legitimate work as a singer, but his attraction to a gangster's moll draws Danny back into the underworld until murder is the only way out.

Presley's orders to report for induction into the army conflicted with Wallis' shooting schedule. Y. Frank Freeman, Paramount's production chief, told Uncle Sam: "Elvis isn't asking for a postponement, but if he is not able to make the picture [then called *Sing You Sinners*], Lichter, *Elvis in Hollywood*, which Paramount has set for January 13, it will cost the studio and Hal Wallis between $300,000 and $350,000 because of preparatory investments. Therefore I plan to ask the Memphis draft board to postpone his induction for eight weeks so we won't lose that large sum of money."

Presley's manager, Tom Parker, said the draft notice cost Elvis half a million in immediate income and the United States government half a million in taxes plus the $78 a month he'd draw as a private.

Dolores Hart, the leading lady of *Loving You*, is back as the pure-at-heart woman who ultimately wins Presley's love. A few years after this picture she became a nun. Born Dolores Hicks (1938), she spent most of her childhood wondering if her parents were ever going to decide

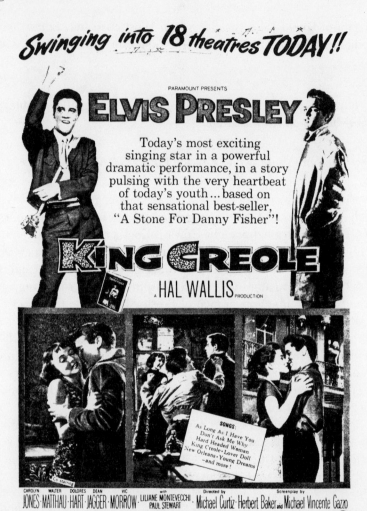

Ad for *King Creole*.

whether to stay married. They were divorced and married so often the church became their second home. In high school Dolores played St. Joan and won a scholarship, and soon after she was on the silver screen. But it all happened too fast. "I keep reminding myself who I really am," she told *Screenland* shortly before she entered the convent. "If Dolores Hart should vanish tomorrow, I want to be very sure that Dolores Hicks still exists."

The Music

Most of the songs are heavily flavored with Dixieland. Presley's "Santa Claus Is Back in Town," an outrageous bumps and grinds number, suggests that Jerry Leiber and Mike Stoller anticipated this project. The Christmas song was recorded in September of 1957; *King Creole* four months later.

"Hard Headed Woman" was the only hit single, issued ahead of time to promote the movie. Only the tail end is heard in the film and Presley is off stage at the time, which was, to say the least, a disappointment. The song originally written for the title, "Danny," was altered slightly and became "Lonely Blue Boy," later a hit for Conway Twitty. An instrumental version of this song can be heard briefly toward the end of the film when Presley sings "As Long as I Have You." "Danny" finally surfaced 21 years later on RCA's "Legendary Performer Volume Three."

Other songs that were deleted include "Banana" by Sid Tepper and Roy C. Bennett and "Turtles, Berries and Gumbo" by Al Wood and Kay Twomey.

Elvis Presley: "King Creole," "New Orleans," "As Long as I Have You," "Lover Doll" (issued on RCA EP soundtrack vol. 1), "Trouble," "Young Dreams," "Crawfish," and "Dixieland Rock" (on RCA EP soundtrack vol. 2), "Hard Headed Woman," "Don't Ask Me Why" (released as RCA single), and "Steadfast, Loyal and True," available on RCA soundtrack LP.

The Reception

"...Presley emerges a more forceful actor in this one, which should be good news to the song stylist's legions of fans."—*Film Daily*.

"Well, the comments on this one were very different. For the most, they don't care for it.... I think that the people who came (mostly teenagers) expected a lot of singing and plenty of happiness, but the show was quite different."—Harry Hawkinson, a Minneapolis exhibitor.

"I predicted from the first that Elvis might make a fair actor someday and I still think so. After he gets out of the Army and is a little more serious in his viewpoint on life, his virility and natural dramatic ability should be welcome in serious roles and he shouldn't have to rock that geetar at all."—*Citizens News*.

"This was SRO on the second night. Here is where you pick up the slack."—Bruce Wendorff, a Montana exhibitor.

"In portraying the rebellious and troubled Danny, Presley gives a performance that hardly offers a challenge to Marlon Brando, but he has come a long way...."—*Motion Picture Herald.*

"Elvis always holds his own here. This one would have been a lot better in color. But business was good anyway."—Sam Elrod, an exhibitor in South Dakota.

"This entangled series of cliches, each with more unlikely motivation than the last, provides the most unattractive Presley vehicle so far."—*Monthly Film Bulletin.*

"Before playing this we were told it's not as good as *Loving You.* Maybe, but at least we were sure of making film rental. That's more than we can say for a lot of the big ones. Play it—you can't go wrong."—Harold Bell, an exhibitor in Quebec.

"In all fairness, Presley does show himself to be a surprisingly sympathetic and believable actor on occasion. He also does some very pleasant, soft and melodious singing, unlike most of his better known work."—*Variety.*

"Presley always does a standout business and this was no exception. Don't believe this picture is quite as good as his last one, but the teenagers don't care as long as Elvis is there."—Harold Smith, an Iowa exhibitor.

". . . Elvis is the surprise of the day. He delivers his lines with good comic timing, considerable intelligence and even flashes of sensitivity. If he's been studying it's paying off handsomely."—*The Los Angeles Times.*

"This is the poorest Presley picture to date, and I guess the paying public smelled it and stayed away."—M.W. Long, an Iowa exhibitor.

". . . Elvis' role requires a certain sensitivity. Surprisingly, he displays flashes of this, if only intermittently to light up the moral problems he faces."—*The Los Angeles Examiner.*

". . . we were pleased with the paying customers it brought in. The teenagers seem to still go for Elvis."—Paul Rickletts, a Kansas exhibitor.

"There's enough rock and rumble plus Presley here to appeal to those who like this type of entertainment. If Presley following is still what it used to be, this one lines up as a successful picture, whose routine story and dialog won't hurt it."—*Motion Picture Exhibitor.*

". . . the Pelvis not only does his personalized bumps and grinds as he belts out a dozen hit tunes, but he also acts well enough to carry a story that holds real suspense for mature audiences."—*Hollywood Reporter.*

The Cast

Elvis Presley (Danny Fisher), Carolyn Jones (Ronnie), Dolores Hart (Nellie), Dean Jagger (Mr. Fisher), Liliane Montevecchi ("Forty" Nina), Walter Matthau (Maxie Fields), Jan Shepard (Mimi), Paul Stewart (Charlie LeGrand), Vic Morrow (Shark), Jack Grinnage (Dummy), Dick Winslow (Eddie Burton), Raymond Bailey (Mr. Evans).

The Credits

Director Michael Curtiz, *Producer* Hal B. Wallis, *Associate Producer* Paul Nathan, *Screenplay* Herbert Baker and Michael Vincente Gazzo, based on the novel *A Stone for Danny Fisher* by Harold Robbins, *Director of Photography* Russell Harlan, A.S.C., *Art Directors* Hal Pereira and Joseph MacMillan, *Assistant Director* Michael Moore, *Sound* Harold Lewis and Charles Frenzbach, *Music* Walter Scharf, *Choreographer* Charles O'Curran, *Editor* Warren Low. B&W VistaVision 115 min. Paramount.

Sources

Boxoffice, Vol. 74, No. 8, December 15, 1958, pg. 18; Vol. 74, No. 7, December 8, 1958, pg. 18; Vol. 74, No. 10, December 29, 1958, pg. 10; Vol. 74, No. 16, February 19, 1959, pg. 10; Vol. 74, No. 20, March 9, 1959, pg. 10; Vol. 75, No. 1, April 27, 1959, pg. 10; Lichter, *Elvis in Hollywood.*

Let's Rock! (1958)

Columbia carried on its tradition of casting ballad singers in the lead of rock movies. In this instance it's Julius La Rosa (born January 2, 1930, in Brooklyn, New York), who got his start on Arthur Godfrey's TV show in the early fifties. "Julius La Rosa will probably have to have his name changed, but he's a cinch for movies—if he wants 'em," claimed an anonymous writer in *Boxoffice.* The writer saw La Rosa as a replacement for Mario Lanza. "Those Lanza film grosses are still

Ad for *Let's Rock!*

uppermost in Hollywood's minds, and Julius is just the boy who can do a reprise at the boxoffice. . . . If he gets to movieland, he'll be a sensation. . . . Let's hope he doesn't make with the Lanza temperament!"

But it was Godfrey that had the temperament. He periodically fired employees for no reason other than to keep the rest in line. He gave La Rosa the shoe right on the air one night and later told the press he'd done it because La Rosa had lost his humility, unaware of the irony of his remark. The publicity boosted La Rosa's career. He'd already had a few minor hits. After the incident with Godfrey he landed his own TV show. But the closest he'd come to rock and roll, prior to his appearance in this film, was when he introduced Don and Phil Everly on his show, and he seemed uncomfortable even with that. His attempts to joke with the boys were an embarrassment, and when he learned they were both younger than his socks, La Rosa lamely told the audience that Pat Boone was old enough to be their grandfather. Mercifully, when he didn't get his anticipated laugh, he left the stage. Having La Rosa's name above the title of *Let's Rock!* creates the perfect oxymoron. As Tommy Adano, La Rosa's career as a pop singer is on the skids until an aspiring female rock and roll composer turns his career around with the big beat. La Rosa's success as a rocker in the film's finale defies all reason.

Biggest drawing card of the film is the appearance of Danny and the Juniors singing "At the Hop," one of the most popular songs of the decade. Danny Rapp (born May 10, 1941), Dave White (September 1940), Frank Maffei (November 1940), and Joe Terranova (January 30, 1941) all hailed from Philadelphia and started singing together during their high school days, when they called themselves the Juvenairs. Arthur Singer, the owner of a small record company, took them under his wing, changed their name and took one of their songs to "American Bandstand's" Dick Clark. Clark liked the record but suggested they change the title from "Do the Bop" to "At the Hop." Singer had a local hit with it on his label, but it wasn't until ABC-Paramount pressed the record that it became a nationwide hit. "Rock and Roll Is Here to Stay" was the group's followup number which sounded too similar to "At the Hop" to have the same impact. After that the group faded away.

"I think when we had our shot in the beginning, if we had been a little more serious about it, we could have done much more with it," Terranova lamented during a 1982 interview with Clark. "I guess we were just regular street kids. We couldn't wait to get home and hang out on the corner."

Danny Rapp committed suicide in 1983.

Another ABC-Paramount group is featured in *Let's Rock!*, singing their only hit, "Short Shorts." The Royal Teens consisted of Bob Gaudio (November 17, 1942), Joe Villa, Tom Austin, Bill Crandall (replaced by Larry Qualaino) and Billy Dalton (replaced by Al Kooper), all from Fort Lee, New Jersey, with the exception of Joe Villa, who hailed from Brooklyn, New York. Bob Gaudio eventually left the group to form the Four Seasons and was responsible for that group's biggest hits. He didn't however, write "Short Shorts."

Roy Hamilton (born April 16, 1929) hailed from Leesburg, Georgia, and was an amateur heavyweight boxer. Disc jockey Bill Cook heard him singing in a small Newark night club and took him to Epic Records. Hamilton had a series of hits on the R&B charts and finally broke into the pop charts with his energetic "Don't Let Go" in 1958. He died of stroke on July 20, 1969. He sings two songs in *Let's Rock!*

Giving Julius La Rosa a run for his money on his own turf was Della Reese from Detroit, Michigan (born July 6, 1932), a former gospel singer with Mahalia Jackson and Clara Ward. She had a hit record, "And That Reminds Me," before signing to do this film, and had an even bigger hit after, "Don't You Know," in 1959.

And as out of place as La Rosa is in a rock movie he has nothing

Top: Danny and the Juniors. Bottom: The Tyrones. From *Let's Rock!*

on disc-jockey-turned-game-show-host Wink (real name Winston Conrad) Martindale from Bells, Tennessee. Now known as Wink Martindale, he got his start in radio when he was sixteen and had a hit record from the religious "Deck of Cards" in 1959.

The Music

Paul Anka: "I'll Be Waiting There for You."
Danny and the Juniors: "At the Hop."
Roy Hamilton: "Here Comes Love."
Julius La Rosa: "Casual," "There Are Times," "Two Perfect Strangers," and "Crazy Crazy Party."
Wink Martindale: "All Love Broke Loose."
Della Reese: "Lonelyville."
The Royal Teens: "Short Shorts."
The Tyrones: "Blast Off," released with "I'm Shook" (label unknown).

The Reception

". . . the script . . . and the direction . . . capture the idiom and mood of today's youth more authentically than any film this reviewer has seen recently." — *The Hollywood Reporter.*

"Name of Julius La Rosa, who makes his film bow, could help the draw, and line-up of name recording gueststars further embellishes musical's possibilities in the teenage market for which it patently is aimed." — *Variety.*

"It will appeal largely to teenagers and those adults interested in rock and roll." — *Hollywood Citizen News.*

"Even if La Rosa could act, and by now it should be sufficiently established that he can't, *Let's Rock!* would still be difficult to endure." — *The Los Angeles Times.*

". . . the plot of this musical is negligible, and the script a mere peg on which to hang a succession of earpiercing rock 'n' roll numbers and ballads. In view of the mechanical, disc-factory deadness of these numbers, the film's somewhat belated contention, that rock is here to stay, remains every bit as resistable as ever." — *British Film Institute.*

"A pretty good little program feature with several good rock 'n' roll numbers in it. It portrays the battle between ballads and rock 'n' roll

Wink Martindale (on stage) hosts a rock 'n' roll party in *Let's Rock!*

with the latter winning over the ballad singing. Had several to complain while the ballads were being sung."—I. Roche, an exhibitor in Florida.

"These films are really bad, but the kids seem to like them. You know your market. There's a rock and roll tune a minute or so, so no fan will be cheated. The groups get progressively worse to an adult's eye and ear so the kids will probably find them progressively better."—*Motion Picture Exhibitor.*

"Where did they dig up this clinker? And what an assortment of oddballs all assembled in one picture. Fair teenage first night, but had an $8.35 total and second night. Skip it, brother exhibitor—it's terrible."—Frank E. Sabin, an exhibitor in Montana.

The Cast

Julius La Rosa (Tommy Adano), Phyllis Newman (Kathy Abbott), Conrad Janis (Charlie), Joy Harmon (pickup girl), Fred Kareman (Monk), Peter Paull (Gordo), Charles Shelander (Clinch), Wink Martindale (himself), Harold Gary (Shep Harris), Jerry Hackady (floor manager), Ned Wertimer (studio manager), Ron McLewdon (engineer), Tony Brande (bartender), Danny and the Juniors (themselves), Paul Anka (himself), Della Reese (herself), Roy Hamilton (himself), The Tyrones (themselves), The Royal Teens (themselves).

The Credits

Producer-Director Harry Foster, *Screenplay* Hal Hackady, *Assistant Director* Ben Berk, *Director of Photography* Jack Etra, *Choreographer* Peter Gennaro, *Art Director* Charles Fawson, *Sound* Edward Johnstone, *Music* Walter Marks. B&W 79 min. Columbia.

Sources

Boxoffice, Vol. 75, No. 15, August 3, 1959, pg. 10; Vol. 75, No. 6, April 27, 1959, pg. 10; *Movie Play,* Vol. 8, No. 1, January 1954, pg. 68; Nite, *Rock On;* Stambler, *Encyclopedia of Pop Rock and Soul;* Terrace, *Complete Encyclopedia of Television Programs.*

Love Me Tender (1956)

The motion picture debut of Elvis Presley, the King of Rock 'n' Roll, had been previously announced by 20th Century–Fox as *The Reno Brothers* (with Cameron Mitchell in the role given to Presley), but with the change of title and star, Fox ordered 550 prints of the film, a record number at the time. In the beginning the folks at Fox had little faith in the singer's longevity, which is why he has a supporting role in a film not tailored to his talents. It is essentially a western melodrama, and the four songs Presley sings are not rock numbers for the simple reason that rock music would have been a little out of place in a Civil War story. (However, the 1987 smash hit *Dirty Dancing,* supposedly set in the 1960s, has anachronistically up-to-date costumes and dance numbers, suggesting that, at the very least, Presley could have done an upbeat version of "Johnny Comes Marching Home.")

The four songs are credited to Vera Matson, the wife of Fox's musical director Ken Darby, who actually wrote them. Darby was no fool. Presley had already had three number one hits (one of them a double-sided hit) and Darby had every reason to believe one or maybe all of the songs from the film would score big too. So he refused to use

Crowds line up for Elvis' film debut in *Love Me Tender*.

Presley's musicians—Scotty Moore, Bill Black and D.J. Fontana—in favor of his own Ken Darby Trio. The title song from the film sold 800,000 copies before it was even pressed. With his wife getting a cut for the writing and Darby's trio taking a share as well, Darby made out like a bandit. "Love Me Tender" was the sixteenth most popular song of the year, and Presley never sounded worse. Frankly, he sounds as if he had a cold.

Born in Tupelo, Mississippi, to a doting mother and a less than ambitious father, Elvis Presley became "The King" not necessarily because he was the best rocker but because his recordings helped pave the way for the black singers who couldn't get air play. Sam Phillips, who owned Sun Records in Memphis, Tennessee, believed he could make a million bucks with a white singer who sounded black. It took Phillips a while to realize that the greasy looking kid with sideburns and a snarl was his dream come true, although he sold his million-dollar dream for $35,000 hard cash. Unable to meet the demand for Presley's records, Phillips sold Presley's contract to Tom Parker, a carny hustler with a phoney "Colonel" tag stuck in front of his name. Parker took his hot new property to RCA Victor, a company with the financial clout to promote the boy into a star. The release of "Heartbreak Hotel," coupled with Presley's appearance on the Dorsey TV show, made "The Hillbilly Cat" a sensation. Presley's facial expressions made the most of every

(Left–right) Elvis Presley, William Campbell, Mildred Dunnock, and Richard Egan. From *Love Me Tender.*

sexual euphemism in his songs, and just in case somebody missed the point he would do the bumps and grinds with his microphone. His appearance on NBC's "Milton Berle Show" caused public outrage.

"It isn't enough to say that Elvis is kind to his parents," said Eddie Condon in the *New York Journal.* "That still isn't a free ticket to behave like a sex maniac in public before millions of impressionable kids." The *Catholic Sun* claimed Presley's "voodoo of frustration and defiance" was morally damaging, and a writer for the *New York Times* expressed his fear that Presley's gyrations might overstimulate twelve-year-olds. In his own defense Presley appeared on Hy Gardner's TV show and remarked: "I don't see that any type of music would have a bad influence on people. It's only a music."

Presley's first RCA album was the biggest selling record in the company's history before it was even pressed, simultaneously divided into six singles, each of which sold in excess of 100,000 copies. There was no question at the time he made *Love Me Tender* that he could sell records. But could he sell movies? The folks at Fox weren't sure.

Assigned to the job of producing the picture was David Weisbart, an ex-film cutter who had recently made the quintessential giant

monster movie of the 1950s, *Them!* and James Dean's most popular film
*Rebel Without a Cause.** The leads were given to two studio contract
players, Richard Egan and Debra Paget. Egan did the film against his
will, not wanting to take a back seat to Presley. His appearance in the
film netted him more fan mail than any other Fox actor at the time. A
dependable, iron-jawed hero, Egan got his start as Joan Crawford's
beleaguered husband in *The Damned Don't Cry* (1950) and remained active until the close of the decade, often in larger-than-life costume
dramas. He was most engaging in *A Summer Place* (1959) and *Pollyanna*
(1960), where he showed signs of more warmth and understanding than
he customarily let on. He finished his career on TV soap operas, claim-
ing that he'd retired from feature films because he didn't want to make
movies that would embarrass his kids. He was married to actress
Patricia Hardy, the leading lady of Sam Katzman's *Don't Knock the Rock*.

In *Love Me Tender* Egan played Vance Reno, Presley's older
brother. Vance is reported dead during the Civil War. His girl Cathy
(Paget) marries his brother Clint (Presley). Vance's surprise return
threatens to break up the marriage. Rather than hurt his brother, Vance
decides to sacrifice his and Cathy's happiness by going away. But before
he can disappear he's jailed for the robbery of a Union train. Vance
realizes he'll be running for the rest of his life if he doesn't return the
loot, but the others involved don't see it that way. They bust Vance out
of jail so he can take them to the money. When they see that Vance is
hell-bent on giving it up, the gang convinces Clint that his brother is
planning to run away with Cathy. Clint wounds Vance, feels remorseful
and is killed saving Vance's life.

Fox issued a story that an alternate ending was being considered
to thwart the possible "adverse public reaction" to Presley's on-screen
death. What remains on film is the ghostly image of Presley, singing a
reprise of the title song, a moment guaranteed to touch the heart of
every Presley fan.

W.A. Windschitl, an exhibitor in Comfrey, Minnesota, said he
hoped that future Presley films would leave him alive at the end of the
show. Windschitl was ready to lock up his theatre when he heard noises
coming from the auditorium and found ten young girls still sobbing.

---

*Weisbart once considered Presley for a James Dean biography. Since Dean was
one of Presley's favorite actors it sounded great to him. He had aspirations of step-
ping into Dean's shoes. But the picture was never made.

"After about ten minutes they left," he said. "I didn't have a tissue left in the house." They came back the following night to weep some more. "The bigger joke," added Windschitl, "was on the married man who walked out ahead of his wife and who was getting a big kick out of the cryers until he turned around to find his own wife red-eyed too."

The picture broke all previous records at a Texas drive-in, and its manager, W.R. Woody, wanted a dozen more like it. "Fox terms were outrageous," said Woody, "but that will not come as a surprise to many exhibitors. Cannot complain, however. We made a batch of jack and did a terrific snack bar business. Even sold a bunch of Elvis Presley hats."

Jealousy and confusion soured the profits made by some exhibitors who just couldn't relate to Presley or his fans. "What's this Elvis got that I haven't got or that I couldn't twist out of shape?" asked one perplexed exhibitor while he counted his biggest take in years.

"Love Me Tender" became the nation's number one song in the month of October, pushing Presley's double-sided hit of "Hound Dog" and "Don't Be Cruel" into the number two slot. It was the first time the same singer held both positions until The Beatles came along almost a decade later.

Coinciding with the premiere of the film at the Carib and Miracle theatres in Florida was the front page story about a group of youngsters who picketed the *Miami Daily News* to protest the paper's entertainment editor, Herb Rau, who consistently spelled Presley's name backwards. The angry crowd carried placards back and forth in front of the building. The cards read: ELVIS HAS GOT IT, HERB RAU SHOULD CATCH IT! HERB, STOP SINKING OUR DREAM BOAT. HERB RAU AIN'T NOTHIN' BUT A HOUN' DAWG. MR. RAU, DON'T YELSERP OUR PRESLEY.

Rau bravely faced the crowd with a sign of his own: I SURRENDER, BUT IT'S STILL YELSERP.

The event was captured on film by (who else?) Fox Movietone News.

At the Essex Theatre in Miami the manager stuck a lifesize photo cut-out of Presley behind his snack bar just to see what would happen. Sales soared.

"What we can't understand," said manager Walton Oakerson, "is how Elvis sold sweets when he looks like he's been eating sour pickles."

Murray Meinberg, the manager of a theatre in Flushing, New York, ran a specially made trailer several weeks prior to booking the film, paid for by the local meat market. It was a shot of Presley with the burning question: "Do you Love Meat Tender?"

"It was a crime to take the merchant's money," Meinberg remarked. "Nothing could have sold our playdate any better."

It seemed that Presley's movie was doing more than just exciting the expectations of his fans; it was also sparking a fire of creative enthusiasm amongst the exhibitors. In Detroit, where a Presley-style hairdo caused one youngster to be suspended from high school, manager Bob Bothwell set up a barber shop in the lobby of his theatre and gave free Presley haircuts. The Warner Theatre in Connecticut offered Presley albums, photos, and six-month passes to the best Presley impersonators. A twelve-year-old in Salt Lake City drew crowds to the Rialto Theatre by lip-synching to Presley records supplied by a sound-truck and a disc jockey. Three radio stations in the city aired programs that argued for and against the singer. Listeners were invited to write in. The best pro–Presley letter won a pair of blue suede shoes. The winner of the con side got a real live hound dog. A Wisconsin theatre held a talent show to find the best Presley clone and in spite of rain the night of the contest the place was packed. One exhibitor ran the movie from 10 a.m. to midnight for five days. "You could hear the music of the old coinchanger working overtime to keep the theatre packed," he remarked, "not only with the younger set, but also with the oldsters who became curious when seeing the continuous line waiting to see the show." He had to hire extra help to man the snack bar.

Before he made the film, Presley told a group of reporters that as far as he knew, he wouldn't be singing in the film. "I took a strict acting test," Presley told them. "Actually, I wouldn't care too much about singing in the movies. I do enough singing around the country." Presley knew he couldn't build a whole career on singing. "Look at Frank Sinatra," he said. "Until he added acting to singing he found himself slipping down hill."

But Elvis did sing in all of his pictures, and after a dozen stinkers he found himself on the defensive. "You can't go beyond your limitation," he said. "They want me to try an artistic picture. That's fine. Maybe I can pull it off one day. But not now. My pictures have all made money. I entertain people with what I do. I'd be a fool to tamper with that kind of success."

Producer Hal Wallis, who once said he'd rather deal with the devil than with Presley's manager, claimed that an Elvis Presley picture was the only guaranteed money maker there was. Which may have been true when he said it, but Presley's vapid formula films, which Wallis triggered with *Blue Hawaii,* eventually disenchanted even the most ardent of his supporters. Presley was forced to return to personal appearances by the late 1960s, but by that time his live performances were no better than his stinky movies. He'd forgotten how to rock. His army of impersonators could have done a better job. Presley waddled across the stage as if he were sleepwalking, passing out scarves while he sang his old songs with about as much vitality as Perry Como. There were fans who remained loyal to the bitter end, even after the singer had become bloated with junk food and his brain fried from years of drugs. One fan who was perceptive enough to know the King was just going through the motions was asked to explain why he wanted to see Presley in concert. The fan replied: "I came to see the man who used to be Elvis Presley."

Officially, Elvis Presley died at 3:30 p.m. on August 16, 1977. But to those who were paying attention, it happened long before that.

The Music

Elvis Presley: "Love Me Tender," "Poor Boy," "Let Me," and "We're Gonna Move," all available on RCA.

The Reception

". . . a good action entry with a story that holds up and would entertain even without the special b.o. gimmick. . . . When not too intent on his acting, Presley has a good screen appearance." — *The Hollywood Reporter.*

"[Presley's] acting — in this, his first picture — is as good as anyone else's." — *Modern Screen.*

"Presley is not this reviewer's idea of an attractive or engaging personality and where he seems sympathetic . . . he does so largely because of the efforts of the director and the good cast. . . ." — *Variety.*

". . . a first-class Western with a good deal of general appeal. . . . [Presley] could very easily depend in future roles on straight talent rather than his now infamous bumps and grinds." — *Motion Picture Herald.*

"Is it a sausage? It is certainly smooth and damp-looking but who ever heard of a 172-lb. sausage 6 ft. tall?... Words occasionally can be made out, like raisins in cornmeal mush.... And then ... a big, trembly tender half smile, half sneer slowly across the CinemaScope screen. The message that millions of U.S. teenage girls love to receive...."—*Time.*

The Cast

Richard Egan (Vance), Debra Paget (Cathy), Elvis Presley (Clint), Robert Middleton (Siringo), William Campbell (Brett), Neville Brand (Mike Gavin), Mildred Dunnock (the mother), Bruce Bennett (Major Kincaid), James Drury (Ray), Russ Conway (Ed Galt), Ken Clark (Kelso), Barry Coe (Davis), L.Q. Jones, Paul Burns, Jerry Sheldon.

The Credits

Director Robert D. Webb, *Producer* David Weisbart, *Screenplay* Robert Buckner, *Story* Maurice Geraghty, *Director of Photography* Leo Tover, *Art Director* Lyle R. Wheeler and Maurice Ransford, *Set Directors* Walter M. Scott and Fay Babcock, *Music* Lionel Newman, *Sound* Alfred Bruzlin and Harry M. Leonard, *Editor* Hugh S. Fowler. B&W, C/S 89 min. 20th Century–Fox.

Sources

Boxoffice, Vol. 70, No. 6, December 1, 1956, pg. 197; Vol. 70, No. 7, December 8, 1956, pg. 303; Vol. 70, No. 9, December 22, 1956, pg. 315; Vol. 70, No. 15, February 2, 1957, pg. 7; Vol. 70, No. 18, February 23, 1957, pg. 11; Vol. 70, No. 19, March 2, 1957, pg. 11; Carr and Farren, *Elvis;* Lichter, *Elvis in Hollywood;* "Mike Connolly's Exclusive Report from Hollywood," May 1957.

Loving You (1957)

This film would more aptly have been called *Loving Elvis* as it was a pretty Technicolor package designed specifically to sell Elvis Presley to middle America. It was produced by Hal Wallis, who'd originally signed Elvis with the intention of giving him the role in *The Rainmaker* that ultimately went to Earl Holliman. Instead Wallis decided to have

Ad for *Loving You.*

director-writer Hal Kanter build a vehicle for Presley. "Teddy Bear," written by the founders of Cameo-Parkway Records (Kal Mann and Bernie Lowe), was a number one hit from the film in the summer of 1957, inspired by the rumor that the singer had a teddy bear collection.

The story is a dandified version of Presley's own rise to fame and the controversy caused by the music he sings. As Deke Rivers, Presley is promoted into stardom by a somewhat ruthless manager played by Lizabeth Scott who pretty much will do whatever it takes to succeed. When Presley finds out she's had to tell a fib or two along the way he's ready to call it quits. Scott forces him to face facts about the business and himself. She got him the break, but it's up to him to take advantage of it—which he does.

The Music

Elvis Presley: "Mean Woman Blues," "(Let Me Be Your) Teddy Bear," "Loving You," "Got a Lot o' Livin' to Do," "Lonesome Cowboy," "Hot Dog" and "Party," available on RCA Soundtrack album. "Teddy Bear" and "Loving You" released as a single. "Loving You," "Party," "Teddy Bear," and "True Love" released on RCA EP *Loving You, Volume 1.* "Lonesome Cowboy," "Hot Dog," "Mean Woman Blues," and "Got a Lot o' Livin' to Do" released on RCA EP *Loving You Volume 2.*

The Reception

"Personally, I find [Presley] interesting when he throbs out numbers like 'Loving You' and 'Mean Woman Blues' and 'Hot Dog.' He is, in his highly personal way, today's youth, and the mistake other studios and mediums have made with him is the one Mr. Wallis' did not make: There is no point in 'editing' this boy."—Ruth Waterbury.

"A real good picture, well made, and well edited. Elvis does a real nice job of singing the title song, and stands still to do it. This is much better than his first effort, better story, more color, better acting."— Paul Ricketts, a Kansas exhibitor.

"The phenomenon of Elvis Presley is one of the more puzzling and less agreeable aspects of modern popular music. Basically a rhythm and blues singer, Presley adopts a slurred and husky style of delivery and a series of grotesque body gestures to impose on his otherwise innocuous material a more suggestive meaning."—*Monthly Film Bulletin.*

Top: Elvis and Dolores Hart. Bottom: Elvis singing "Let's Have a Party." From *Loving You.*

"Another Presley natural. Color is the best. No one should pass this as it will guarantee extra business."—D. Ellickson, a Wisconsin exhibitor.

"Hal Kanter and Herbert Baker have written some funny lines and situations, many of which were completely lost at the press screening ... young girls, and some not so young, set up ear-splitting screams almost every time Presley appeared on screen. It might be a good idea for the next such screening to be held in the vaults at Fort Knox."—*The Hollywood Reporter*.

"Supposed to be his best picture. Business good, so I'll not press my luck on another, as I figure we've had it."—Frank E. Sabin, a Montana exhibitor.

". . . attempts pretty largely to play upon the juvenile mob spirit which has marked so much of the Presley experience. But one has the feeling that it is very much of an effort to warm up a rather chilled banquet at best."—Edwin Schallert.

"Personally, I didn't think much of it; but they come, so who's right?"—Peter Ubertino, an Alabama exhibitor.

". . . though the rock 'n' roll craze has hit its peak, there's no question that a sizable part of the citizenry will welcome Presley back for his second screen appearance."—*Variety*.

"The picture did capacity business the whole territory, and England was no exception. SRO during its run here."—Terry Axley, an Arkansas exhibitor.

"To be true to its own brand of ballyhoo, the film would have to show Elvis—modest and shy fellow that he is—rejecting all offers to lend himself to Hollywood commercialism."—*Time*.

The Cast

Elvis Presley (Deké Rivers), Lizabeth Scott (Glenda Markle), Wendell Corey (Tex Warner), Dolores Hart (Susan Jessup), James Gleason (Carl), Ralph Dumke (Tallman), Paul Smith (Skeeter), Ken Becker (Wayne), Jana Lund (Daisy).

The Credits

Director Hal Kanter, *Producer* Hal B. Wallis, *Screenplay* Herbert Baker and Hal Kanter from a story by Agnes Thompson, *Director of*

Photography Charles Lang, Jr., A.S.C., *Art Director* Hal Pereira and Albert Nozaki, *Assistant Director* James Rosenberger, *Editor* Howard Smith, A.C.E., *Music* Walter Scharf. C/VistaVision 101 min. Paramount.

Sources

Boxoffice, Vol. 72, No. 21, March 17, 1958, pg. 13; Vol. 71, No. 23, September 28, 1957, pg. 12; Vol. 72, No. 10, December 28, 1957, pg. 13; Bronson, *Billboard Book of Number One Hits.*

Mister Rock and Roll (1957)

Mister Rock and Roll was the title disc jockey Alan Freed awarded to himself for coining the term. Independently made and released by Paramount, the movie once again depicts Freed as rock music's number one crusader, battling almost insurmountable odds to bring rock and roll to the people who love it. In this film he organizes a rock program to raise money for medical research. The issue of personal gain never enters these fantasies of Freed's. He does what he does because he loves the music.

The best thing about Freed's movies was the way the songs were set in blocks, usually as many as five in a row, simulating one of Freed's famous live stage shows. Many of the performers from *Rock, Rock, Rock* appeared in this film. New additions included Brook Benton, Ferlin Husky and Clyde McPhatter.

Brook Benton (born Benjamin Franklin Peay on September 19, 1931) didn't really click until a year after he appeared in *Mister Rock and Roll.* He was traveling with a spiritual group until he met songwriter Clyde Otis. They wrote hits for Nat Cole and Clyde McPhatter before Benton scored with "It's Just a Matter of Time." His last big hit was "Rainy Night in Georgia" in 1970. He lives in New York with his family and has returned to gospel music.

Clyde McPhatter, who had a hit record with the Benton-Otis song "A Lover's Question," also started as a gospel singer. From Durham, North Carolina, McPhatter was the son of a Baptist minister. He was still in his teens when he sang lead tenor for Billy Ward and the Dominoes. In 1953 McPhatter was fired by Ward, so he formed his own group, The Drifters. He was drafted in '54 and when he returned from the army he went solo. He died in 1972 from a heart attack.

Ad for *Mister Rock and Roll.*

Top: Screamin' Jay Hawkins' sequence was deleted from *Mister Rock and Roll* because it ridiculed blacks. Bottom: The Moonglows in *Mister Rock and Roll*.

Ferlin Husky was a disc jockey in Bakersfield, California, before he signed with Capitol records in 1957. His first record, "Gone," was the biggest hit he ever had. He hailed from Missouri, born December 3, 1927, and can be seen in *Country Music Holiday* (1958), *Las Vegas Hillbillies* (1966) and *Hillbillies in a Haunted House* (1967).

The Music

La Vern Baker: "Love Me Right (in the Morning)" and "Humpty Dumpty Heart."

Brook Benton: "If Only I Had Known" and "Your Love Alone."

Chuck Berry: "La Juanda" and "Oh Baby Doll," available on Chess.

Shaye Cogan: "Pathway to Sin" and "Get Acquainted Waltz."

Al Fisher and Lou Marks: "Sing Song Siren."

Lionel Hampton: "Mister Rock and Roll," "Hey Poppa Rock," "Hello Folks," "Drum Hi!," and "Star Rocket."

Ferlin Husky: "This Moment of Love" and "Make Me Live Again."

Frankie Lymon and The Teenagers: "Fortunate Fella" and "Love Put Me Out of My Head."

Clyde McPhatter: "Rock and Cry" and "You'll Be There."

The Moonglows: "Barcelona Rock" and "Confess It to Your Heart."

Lois O'Brien: "It's Simply Heavenly."

Teddy Randazzo: "I Was the Last One to Know," "I'll Stop Anything I'm Doing," "Kiddio" (available on Mercury), "Perfect for Love."

Little Richard: "Lucille."

NOTE: "This Moment of Love," "Make Me Live Again," "If Only I Had Known," "Your Love Alone," "It's Simply Heavenly," "Rocky's Love Song," "I Was the Last One to Know," "I'll Stop Anything I'm Doing," "Kiddio," "Perfect for Love," "Rock and Cry," "You'll Be There," and "Keep A-Knockin'" (which is not sung in the film although it may have been shot) comprised the VIK soundtrack album.

The Reception

". . . a natural for any situation catering to teenagers, the young-at-heart, or the musically inclined."—*Motion Picture Herald*.

"This had it. Plenty of rock that helped the teenagers roll into the ticket window. Business good."—D.W. Trisko, an exhibitor in Texas.

"Evidently working from the presumption that if you've got a bad thing don't let it go away, Paramount studio — of all concerns — has perpetuated still another of those rock and roll 'films.'" — *The Los Angeles Times.*

"Played this one New Year's Eve midnight, which gave me extra business, mostly teenagers. This one should have been in color. They should all be in color nowadays." — James Hardy, an exhibitor in Indiana.

". . . has the artistic impact of an animated jukebox — but not very animated." — *Variety.*

"This was okay, but did not do the business that the other rock and rollers have done." — S.T. Jackson, an exhibitor in Alabama.

"Teens will snicker at the antics of some of their favorite singers, who aren't at their best on the screen." — *Hollywood Citizens News.*

The Cast

Alan Freed (himself), Rocky Graziano (himself), Teddy Randazzo (himself), Lois O'Brien (Carol Hendricks), Jay Barney (Joe Prentiss), Al Fisher (Larry), Lou Marks (Lou), Earl George (Leo), Ralph Stantly (station rep).

The Credits

Director Charles Dubin, *Producers* Ralph Serpe and Howard B. Kreitsek, *Screenplay* James Blumgarten, *Director of Photography* Morris Hartzban, *Associate Producer* George Justin, *Choreographer* Roye Dodge, *Assistant Director* Jack Grossberg, *Editor* Angie Ross, *Music* Lionel Hampton. B&W 86 min. A Paramount release.

Sources

Boxoffice, Vol. 72, No. 18, February 24, 1958, pg. 12; Vol. 72, No. 20, March 10, 1958, pg. 13; Vol. 73, No. 5, May 26, 1958, pg. 12; Berry, *Chuck Berry;* Nite, *Rock On;* Pareles and Romanowski, *Rolling Stone Encyclopedia of Rock & Roll.*

Rock All Night (1957)

The second of two rock movies made by producer-director Roger Corman, *Rock All Night* is curiously short on music and has nothing whatsoever to do with teenagers. Advertised by American International in their usual deceptive manner *("Some have to dance . . . some have to kill!"),* this incredible departure from formula strongly tempts the thought that director Corman was out of touch with his audience. The story concerned a group of people held hostage in a sleazy nightclub by a couple of robbers on the lam for the murder of a liquor store owner. They are eventually subdued by a smart-mouthed punk with a chip on his shoulder, played by Dick Miller, a Corman regular.

Ad for *Rock All Night.*

"I remember a lot about *Rock All Night,"* said Miller, "because it was my first starring role." Miller made a deal with AIP's Jim Nicholson and Sam Arkoff to go in halvsies on a full page ad for the actor in *Variety.* The two moguls were furious when the ad appeared with the following quote from *Variety:* "Only the performance of Dick Miller in the lead keeps the audience's interest in the film from disintegrating."

At the time this picture went into release, Jim Nicholson and Sam Arkoff had been in the motion picture business for three years, an independent operation that stayed in business by supplying exhibitors with double feature packages for a bargain price. "These pictures were merchandise," said Arkoff, the company's vice-president. "That's the way we operated. Most of the stuff we did were originals. Why? Because they had to be to fit the concept, which had already been set. We had the concept and the art work. Then we did the script which had to follow the title, the concept or the artwork and also the fact that we were going to make it for a price. Which meant that we couldn't have 1000 moves because we couldn't afford 1000 moves. And we couldn't afford this and we couldn't afford that. So the scripts were more or less written to order by knowledgeable people."

Rock All Night was developed when AIP signed The Platters, the most popular singing group in the world at the time. They began as a

Mel Welles as Sir Bop in *Rock All Night*.

quartet—Tony Williams, Herbert Reed, David Lynch and Alex Hodge. Their manager, Buck Ram, insisted they add Zola Taylor shortly after they signed with Mercury. Disc jockey Bob Salter premiered their first recording, "Only You," in the Seattle area after hearing it on Hunter Hancock's radio show. Hancock's secretary was Tony Williams' wife. Initially the group had been foisted on Mercury as part of a package deal. When "Only You" was originally released it was on Mercury's purple label, indicating that the record was rhythm and blues, but it was reissued a few months later on Mercury's standard black label. One hit record followed another until 1959, when the four male members of the group were busted for smoking dope and consorting with soiled women. Radio stations refused to play their records, and the group never recovered. Lead singer Tony Williams left to go solo, and Mercury Records sued them all for breach of contract (a suit that was ultimately dropped). Buck Ram still holds a copyright on the group's name and various incarnations of the group appear now and then, but Tony Williams is retired in New York, Zola Taylor and Paul Robi are in the Los Angeles area somewhere, Herb Reed is in Georgia singing with his own group, and David Lynch died of cancer in 1981. When they agreed to appear in *Rock All Night* (their last film appearance together), it was for a week's work. The project was given to Corman, who quickly bought a half-hour teleplay called "The Little Guy" which Corman had seen on Jane Wyman's TV show. It was given to Charles Griffith to expand; the focus of the story shifted to center around The Platters. But a last-minute change in the group's concert schedule the day before production meant they would only be available for a day. Griffith rewrote the script accordingly so all of The Platters' scenes could be shot in a day.

"I had a fight scene at the beginning of the picture," Dick Miller recalled, "where this guy named Burt Nelson carries me out of the place. His girlfriend had given him this gold chain that I completely destroyed. I accidentally put my arm through it and turned it into a two foot chain. It looked like a hanger or something."

Nelson played a bouncer, his real-life occupation. Later he went to Europe and opened an Italian restaurant in Berlin.

The movie was completed in five days, shot on left-over sets, like many of AIP's films.

"We won a number of awards," said Sam Arkoff, "'Showmen of the Year' and all that kind of jazz. At conventions people used to get up, meaning to praise us, and say things like, 'You know these pictures don't play in our A theatres but they really make the money.' Which really wasn't true. We did play their A theatres because they couldn't always get a so-called A picture. The *Vagabond King* kind of picture didn't always last. . . . Obviously, there were a lot of our pictures that weren't that great, but there were an awful lot of them that merchandised extremely well." Of all of the producers and directors that Arkoff worked with during the company's 25 years in business, he admired Corman the most. "Roger could move. You toss him in the air and he came down on his feet. He didn't take forever and he wasn't pompous."

Corman eventually headed his own company, New World Pictures and later Concorde/New Horizons, continuing the AIP tradition of hit and run productions.

The Music

The Blockbusters: "Rock All Night," "I Wanna Rock Now," and "Rock and Roll Guitar."

Nora Hayes (singing for Abby Dalton): "The Great Pretender" and "I Guess I Won't Hang Around Here Anymore."

The Platters: "He's Mine" and "I'm Sorry." All the songs were released on a Mercury soundtrack album.

The Reception

"Extremely mediocre, and drawing unintended guffaws at its matinee bow here yesterday, [it] is being packaged as a double-bill with *Dragstrip Girl. . . .* Only the performance (very good, especially considering the so-so-production and direction) of Dick Miller in the lead keeps the audience's interest in the film from disintegrating."—*Variety.*

"Well, here's a switch. This one starts out as a rock and roll movie and ends as a crime story. It's certainly different and the audience was well-pleased with it. . . . All we need is a rock and roll horror film."—Stan Farnsworth, an exhibitor in Nova Scotia.

"Charles B. Griffith has contributed a good script for this type of story, with some funny lines and amusing characterizations. . . . Two groups, the Blockbusters and the Platters, are used for good value."—*Hollywood Reporter.*

"I think they must have made this picture in one day, but even at that it's better than some that take a month."—Victor Webber, an exhibitor in Arkansas.

"Played this on a triple bill and was very glad we did, as it is nothing compared to *Shake, Rattle and Rock.* After seeing this, it hurts the rest of the rock and rollers to follow."—Harold Bell, an exhibitor in Quebec.

"Rock and roll may be dying some places, but not here yet. Above average business for Tues/Wed and only a fair show."—Terry Auxley, an exhibitor in Arkansas.

The Cast

Dick Miller (Shorty), Abby Dalton (Julie), The Platters (themselves), The Blockbusters (themselves), Robin Morse (Al), Richard Cutting (Steve), Bruno Ve Sota (Charlie), Chris Alcaide (Angie), Mel Welles (Sir Bop), Barboura Morris (Syl), Clegg Hoyt (Marty), Russell Johnson (Jigger), Jonathan Haze (Joey), Richard Carlan (Jerry), Jack De Witt (Philippe), Burt Nelson (bartender), Beach Dickerson (the kid), Ed Nelson (Pete).

The Credits

Producer-Director Roger Corman, *Executive Producer* James H. Nicholson, *Screenplay* Charles B. Griffith based on "The Little Guy" by David P. Harmon, *Director of Photography* Floyd Crosby, *Editor* Frank Sullivan, *Art Director* Robert Kinoshita, *Property Master* Karl Brainard, *Key Grip* Charles Hanawalt, *Music* Curly Batson and Buck Ram, *Sound* Robert Post. B&W 65 min. A Sunset Production. An American-International Picture.

Sources

Boxoffice, Vol. 71, No. 24, October 12, 1957, pg. 12; Vol. 73, No. 25, October 13, 1958, pg. 4; Vol. 72, No. 11, January 6, 1958, pg. 13; Vol. 72, No. 14, January 27, 1958, pg. 13; Bronson, *Billboard Book of Number One Hits;* Uslan and Solomon, *Dick Clark's The First 25 Years of Rock & Roll.*

Rock Around the Clock (1956)

This was the first rock movie and the title of the first rock record to reach the top of the charts, sung by Bill Haley, the film's star attraction. Made on a low budget by Sam Katzman, an expert in bargain basement productions, the movie is a fictionalized account of Haley's rise to stardom.

Born William John Clifton Haley in Highland Park, Michigan, on July 6, 1925, Haley entered the music world when he was 13, playing guitar with local bands. He'd come from a musical family. His mother played the piano; his father played the banjo. At 18 Haley had already been on the road with a group called the Down Homers and had cut his first record, "Candy Kisses." Soon after he formed his own band, The Saddlemen, and got a gig at a Chester, Pennsylvania, radio station.

"We started out as a country-western group, then added a touch of rhythm and blues," Haley said. "It wasn't something we planned, it just evolved. We got to where we weren't accepted as country-western or rhythm and blues. It was hard to get bookings for a while. We were something different, something new. We didn't call it that at the time, but we were playing rock 'n' roll."

Haley and the Saddlemen got a contract with Essex Records and cut a version of "Rocket 88." (The original version by the Ike Turner

is considered by many to be the first rock and roll record.) Haley changed the name of his group to the Comets and recorded "Dance with the Dolly," "Patty Cake," "Crazy Man, Crazy," and "Rock This Joint," to little effect. Even "Rock Around the Clock" drew little notice on its first time around. The song was written by Max C. Freedman, a postal employee, and Jimmy De Knight, a pseudonym for the song's publisher, Jim Myers. By the time it came to Haley's attention another singer, Sunny Dae, had already recorded it, but the record flopped. Myers said Haley was supposed to record the song in 1953, but Haley was signed with Dave Miller at Holiday Records and Miller wouldn't let Haley do the song because Miller had a beef with Myers. A year later, after his contract with Miller expired, Haley went to Milt Gabler at Decca Records and recorded "Rock Around the Clock," with "Thirteen Women" for the flip side. (Other sources say Haley went directly from Essex to Decca.) The record did about as well for Haley as it had for Sunny Dae. Haley had better luck with a cover version of Joe Turner's "Shake, Rattle and Roll." Turner's lyrics were spruced up a bit, taking out as much of the sex as possible. Haley didn't want to sing anything that "couldn't be sung in my home or at a church festival."

Ad for *Rock Around the Clock*.

Top: Bill Haley and His Comets. Bottom: Haley teaches Lisa Gaye the guitar. From *Rock Around the Clock*.

He didn't believe it was necessary to write lewd lyrics for the songs to sell. It wasn't until "Rock Around the Clock" was heard behind the titles of MGM's hard-hitting drama about juvenile delinquency in the public school system, *Blackboard Jungle* (1955), that it finally caught the public's attention. By July of that year the song was the best-selling record in the nation and in no time became a national anthem for the young. Haley followed with a succession of hits—"See You Later, Alligator," "R-O-C-K," "Rip It Up"—but never again had the impact of the Freedman/De Knight song.

Unfortunately, *Blackboard Jungle* caused quite a stink. Columnist Hedda Hopper called it the most brutal film she had ever seen. U.S. Ambassador Clare Booth Luce threatened to cause "the greatest scandal in motion picture history!" if the film wasn't withdrawn from the Venice Film Festival. A writer for the *Los Angeles Times* was worried about the picture falling into Communist hands. School board P.R. men said they were shocked by the film's gross exaggeration, while the teachers applauded the film's honesty. By the time the smoke had cleared rock music was forever linked with juvenile delinquency.

"Rock Around the Clock" had been a number one record by the time Sam Katzman hired Haley to appear in his film. Katzman was one of the few filmmakers around who could make a movie quickly enough to capitalize on passing fads. He'd been making short-schedule movies for over two decades, at first for his own company, Victory Pictures. Later, with Jack Dietz, Katzman made a series of horror melodramas with Bela Lugosi and comedies starring the East Side Kids, often combining the two. At Columbia Katzman was given the nickname "Jungle Sam" because of his Jungle Jim series with Johnny Weissmuller, who'd become too heavy to play Tarzan. Katzman's *Superman* serial was so popular in South America that audiences sat through all five hours in one sitting. Katzman made a variety of films at Columbia—westerns, science fiction melodramas, costumers—but none had been more successful than Jungle Jim. That is, until *Rock Around the Clock* grossed four times what Katzman or anyone at Columbia expected it to. When Katzman signed a new contract with Columbia in 1952, he'd just begun to look to fads and headlines for his inspiration. *A Yank in Korea* (1951) was in theatres a few months after the outbreak of the Korean war. Yet Katzman's subsequent films stayed with the traditional genres.

"We got underwater stuff and we got overwater stuff and we got those three characters in the fiery furnace and on top of that we got Linda Christian doing her first screen dance," Katzman off-handedly told a reporter from *Time* who came to the set of Katzman's *Slaves of Babylon* (1953). Katzman said a lot of his films were remakes. *A Yank in Korea* had been a remake of *A Yank in the R.A.F.* (1941). He would eventually remake *Rock Around the Clock* as *Twist Around the Clock* (1961). Katzman added: "We got a new generation, but they got the same old glands."

Katzman was unknown to the world at large, but to the people working in films his name was synonymous with sleaze. Actor Turhan Bey, who had once enjoyed a successful career at Universal, was excited about the prospect of working with actress Gloria Grahame (who had just won an Oscar for her performance in 1952's *The Bad and the Beautiful*) until Bey learned *Prisoners of the Casbah* (1953) was a Katzman cheapie. Columbia boss Harry Cohn once tried to break his contract with Lucille Ball by threatening to put her in Katzman's *The Magic Carpet* (1951) opposite actor John Agar. Miss Ball foiled Cohn by accepting the role. (Agar was almost killed when the wires of his magic carpet broke, leaving him hanging 30 feet above the ground.) There's more than one account of Katzman tearing pages out of scripts to keep his directors on schedule. And if the subject of quality reared its ugly head, Katzman quickly changed the channel. "If you were to X-ray every Oscar you'd find an ulcer in every one of them," he often quipped. Quality isn't a subject that people who never achieve it, or even try to achieve it, like to talk about. Sam got his awards from the bank. He wasn't interested in Oscars.

As *Rock Around the Clock* went into production, Katzman's wife, Hortense, filed a petition in Superior Court, charging Sam with cruelty. She asked for alimony and support for their son, Jerome. Since she remained with Sam until his death in 1973, one assumes they patched things up.

In Katzman's film, Bill Haley is discovered by a down-and-out promoter named Steve Hollis. Hollis takes Haley and his band to New York where, with a little help from real-life disc jockey Alan Freed, Haley becomes a star. Freed, who plays himself, was one of rock music's biggest supporters, credited with giving the music its name. Jim Myers claimed it was "Rock Around the Clock" that inspired Freed. "He put it on the air," said Myers, "and after it was over he said, 'That's got a kind of a rockin' motion, hasn't it? Rolling,' he said, 'like rock and roll.' I said,

'You said it, Alan.'" (Quote from ABC's wonder "Our World" series.) Actually, Freed lifted the phrase from old rhythm and blues records, where it was used as a euphemism for fornication.

Everywhere the picture played it raked in the money. A Michigan exhibitor played it three times in five months, and each time his customers wanted to know when he could run it again. He thought Columbia should let him keep the print and save the shipping costs.

In Texas a drive-in theatre owner parked a pickup truck in the middle of town with posters plastered all over it and a sign that read: "All you cats who want to rock, free bop session at the Crescent Drive-In, Thursday, Friday, Saturday nights." With the bop and a screening of *Rock Around the Clock* the drive-in saw more action than it had seen in years. A Minneapolis theatre owner was so certain he'd have a good crowd, in spite of his traditionally bad December period, he bet his janitor a lunch. And lost. But he was the exception. "We played [it] once, then played it twice (only a month apart) and likely will play it once again if the youngsters keep pleading," said one enthusiastic exhibitor. "Frankly, the teenagers were so enthusiastic that they got the personnel in the snack bar sort of swaying and rocking, too."

They were swaying and rocking outside of a theatre in London, too, blocking traffic and throwing beer bottles. The police were called in to restore order. The crowd got so rowdy after another London showing the police were forced to turn a hose on them. The movie was banned in several communities. In the areas that did allow it the volume was kept low in the hope of curbing excitement. Wanting to know what all the hubbub was about, Queen Elizabeth II cancelled a showing of *The Caine Mutiny* at the Balmoral Castle in Scotland where the Royal Family was vacationing and asked for a print of Katzman's film instead.

In Oslo, a group of overzealous Norwegians swarmed through the downtown section of the city after seeing the movie demanding "More rock! More rock!" The military arrived demanding "More order! More order!" The manager of the theatre could shed little light on the cause of the disruption, except to say that he didn't think the picture was to blame.

"It's American folk music—based on Negro folk tunes—differing from our western music, which stems from European song," observed Edgar Goth, the advertising director for the Stanley Warner Theatres in New Jersey. Goth and a couple of his buddies decided to stage some rock and roll shows to help promote the film. Bill Haley was on hand

to judge a dance contest at the film's opening in Philadelphia where high school students competed for a $25 prize. The place was packed. It didn't take a genius to figure the picture warranted a sequel. That same year Haley was back in Katzman's *Don't Knock the Rock!* with a different group of Comets.

The original Comets were John Grande (accordion and piano), Billy Williamson (steel guitar), Rudy Pompelli (sax), Al Rex (bass), Francis Beecher (Spanish guitar), and Don Raymond (later replaced by Ralph Jones on drums). Haley would periodically hire new Comets on the correct assumption that it was he the audience came to see. But his popularity quickly declined as sexier and more energetic performers emerged on the rock and roll scene. Plump and balding, Haley couldn't compete. A few months after *Don't Knock the Rock!* went into release, Haley went to England, where his arrival created the kind of hysteria he never encountered in the States. Grateful fans, hungry for rock, turned out en masse to welcome him and there followed a panic. A writer for the *Daily Express* said the fans were "tossed like jetsam in the swaying human tide" until their ecstasy turned to fear, "faces bewildered like faces in the panic scenes of Russian films." Seats were smashed at concert halls across the continent wherever Haley played. He continued to play to capacity crowds in Britain well into the 1970s.

In August of 1968, Haley signed a contract with Sonet Grammofon in Stockholm during his tour of Sweden. The records that resulted were unsuccessful, but a year later, at a rock and roll revival show in New York City, an appreciative audience gave Haley an eight-minute ovation. It was Haley's last real moment in the spotlight until 1986 when he was posthumously inducted into the Rock 'n' Roll Hall of Fame. The years before his death in 1981 were not happy ones. He drank too much and became a recluse. "He would talk about his life in the Marine Corps, which he was never in," his eldest son, Jack remarked. "He said he was a deputy sheriff down there in Texas, which he wasn't."

Haley wanted to be recognized as the father of rock and roll, and according to L.A. band manager Steve Brigati, maybe he should be. "Roy Brown predated him with rock. Elvis Presley was better looking. Chuck Berry was more creative. But Bill was the first guy who really got it all across."

Record sleeve (top) and sheet music for "Rock Around the Clock."

The Music

Bill Haley and His Comets: "Rock Around the Clock," "Happy Baby," "Rock-a-Beatin' Boogie," "Razzle Dazzle," "A.B.C. Boogie," "Mambo Rock," "Rudy's Rock," "R-O-C-K," and "See You Later, Alligator." All but the last three numbers were released on subsequent Decca records.

Freddie Bell and His Bellboys: "Giddy Up Ding Dong" and "We're Gonna Teach You to Rock."

Tony Martinez and His Band: "Codfish and Potatoes," "Sad and Lonely," "Cuero," and "Mambo Capri."

The Platters: "The Great Pretender" and "Only You," available on Mercury Records.

The Reception

"It contrasts heady rhythms of rock and roll with the musty atmosphere of booking agency intrigue, and in this instance the rhythm comes out on top. Some clever lines and fast paced plot that doesn't intrude too much on the music...." — *The Los Angeles Times.*

"Speaking as an admittedly middle-aged square, I still have to say that I found this off-beat, low budget, black and white musical thoroughly entertaining. In theaters catering to bobby-soxers and hepcats, it should have the joint really jumping." — *The Hollywood Reporter.*

"... will not only draw hep-cats and teenagers, but people of all ages who love good rock and roll rhythm." — *The Los Angeles Examiner.*

"... speaks the teenager idiom and will prove a handy entry for exhibitors picking a show aimed at the sweater-levi trade. It takes off to a bouncy title beat and never lets up for 76 minutes of foot-patting entertainment." — *Variety.*

"Every teenager in town will be on hand to see this one when you play it.... A well-made rock show that will rock the aisles of your theatre and make you feel good when the show is over." — Robert Klinge, Montana exhibitor.

"This show sure did have the kids dancing in the aisles and it did happen on a Thursday night, which really caused a panic, but was enjoyed by all." — L.J. Bennett, Illinois exhibitor.

"... is a cut above many of the items [Sam Katzman] turns out for the B-picture market under the Clover label and Fred F. Sears has handled the directorial assignment competently." — *Film Daily.*

The Cast

Bill Haley (himself), The Platters (themselves), Tony Martinez (himself), Freddie Bell (himself), Alan Freed (himself), Johnny Johnston (Steve Hollis), Alix Talton (Corinne Talbot), Lisa Gaye (Lisa Johns), John Archer (Mike Dennis), Henry Slate (Corny LaSalle), Earl Barton (Jimmy Johns).

The Credits

Director Fred F. Sears, *Producer* Sam Katzman, *Story & Screenplay* Robert E. Kent and James B. Gordon, *AD* Gene Anderson, Jr., *Director of Photography* Benjamin H. Kline, A.S.C., *Art Director* Paul Palmentola, *Editors* Saul A. Goodkind, A.C.E. and Jack W. Ogilvie, A.C.E., *Set Director* Sidney Clifford, *Choreographer* Earl Barton, *Sound* Josh Westmoreland, *Music Supervisor* Fred Karger. B&W 76 min. A Clover Production. A Columbia Picture.

Sources

Boxoffice, Vol. 68, No. 21, March 17, 1956, pg. 92; Vol. 69, No. 14, July 28, 1956, pg. 11 and 96; Vol. 69, No. 15, August 4, 1956, pg. 11; Vol. 69, No. 16, August 11, 1956, pg. 11; Vol. 69, No. 22, September 22, 1956, pg. 11; Vol. 69, No. 23, September 29, 1956, pg. 11; Vol. 69, No. 24, October 6, 1956, pg. 11; Vol. 69, No. 25, October 13, 1956, pg. 11; Vol. 70, No. 1, October 27, 1956, pg. 11; Vol. 70, No. 2, November 3, 1956, pg. 11; Vol. 71, No. 2, May 4, 1957, pg. 22; Herman, *Rock 'n' Roll Babylon;* Hilburn, "Farewell to Bill Haley"; White, *Rock Stars.*

Rock Around the World (1957)

This British import was originally titled *The Tommy Steele Story.* Tommy Steele probably sings the bulk of the numbers listed, but the film was unavailable for screening and what little information is listed here comes from the memory of R.J. Robertson, who is getting quite senile.

Steele (real name Thomas Hicks, born December 17, 1936), was an energetic, sandy-haired lad who was touted as England's answer to Elvis Presley. As his name had no value in America at the time, American International gave this film a more marketable title (the film isn't much

That's Tommy Steele in the musical sweater. He was England's Elvis Presley.
From *Rock Around the World.*

of a biography anyway) and tacked on an introduction by American disc
jockey Hunter Hancock, who explained that rock and roll was becoming an international phenomenon. The film climaxes with Steele thank-
ing his fans by putting on a big show featuring "his friends," mostly older
jazz artists and folk-skiffle groups. Steele performs "Elevator Rock" with
sing-along lyrics printed on the screen. The film was quite popular in
England. There's a photo of Eddie Fisher and Debbie Reynolds attend-
ing the premiere during their visit to England.

In Hobart, on the island province of Tasmania, an exhibitor
screened the film for the representatives of all the music houses, dance
bands, radio stations and newspapers two months ahead of the opening
date. The stations started playing Steele's records and a rock and roll
contest was held. There was no report on the results.

The Music

"Freight Train," "Doomsday Rock," "Elevator Rock," "Time to
Kill," "Two Eyes," "Will It Be You?" "Build Up," "I Like Take Me Back,

Baby," "You Gotta Go," "Water, Water," "A Handful of Songs," "Cannibal Pot," "Teenage Party," "Butterfingers," and "15 Cents."

Nancy Whiskey sings "Freight Train" and Tommy Steele sings "A Handful of Songs" and "Elevator Rock."

Although Steele never really posed the slightest threat to Presley (or Pat Boone for that matter), he achieved a burst of stardom in *Half a Sixpence* (1967), which led to his being signed by Walt Disney.

The Reception

"Producers . . . wisely mixed in a good portion of other types of music such as calypso and several brands of jazz. . . . [Tommy Steele's] a good entertainer with a very non-revolting style. One can watch him and not feel shame. He gyrates like an unbalanced top but it's good clean fun." — *Los Angeles Times.*

"At first we were timid, as this was made in England and English pictures generally don't do well. But, as this is rock and roll all the way, it's okay." — Harold Bell, a Quebec exhibitor.

"Technically, pic is jerry-built and reflects cheap production standards. Numbers recorded at a London teenage bash are used through pic in other contexts, but are easily recognizable by distinctive tonal quality and poor lip sync." — *Variety.*

". . . it's been crudely Americanized for local consumption by adding intro footage by Yank dee-jay Hunter Hancock. However, it remains emphatically British in concept and largely in locale, even if more in the Cockney than the stiff-upper-lip tradition." — *Hollywood Reporter.*

"All in all, the picture probably does fairly well by those who like this kind of musical." — *Los Angeles Examiner.*

The Cast

Tommy Steele (himself), Patrick Westwood (Brushes), Charles Lamp (Mr. Steele), Peter Lewiston (John Kennedy), John Boxer (Paul Lincoln), Mark Daly (junkshop man), Lisa Daniely (hospital nurse), Bryan Coleman (hospital doctor), Cyril Chamberlain (chief steward), Bernard Hunter (Busker), Alan Weighell (first Steelman), Dennis Price (second Steelman), Leo Polilini (third Steelman), Alan Stuart (fourth Steelman), Tom Littlewood (judo instructor).

The Credits

Director Gerard Bryant, *Producer* Herbert Smith, *Screenplay* Norman Hudis, *Director of Photography* Peter Hennessy, *Editor* Ann Chegwidden, *Art Director* Eric Saw. B&W 71 min. Anglo-Amalgamated/American International.

Sources

Boxoffice, Vol. 73, No. 5, May 26, 1958, pg. 125; Vol. 73, No. 11, July 7, 1958, pg. 4; Jenkinson and Warner, *Celluloid Rock.*

Rock Baby Rock It (1957)

This extremely low budget film was made in Memphis, Tennessee. It received very little in the way of distribution. The story is simple: a group of teens put on a show to raise the rent money for their clubhouse. Apparently the producers hoped Kay Wheeler would help sell the film simply because she had one of the first Elvis Presley fan clubs.

The Music

The Bellew Twins: "Love Me Baby" and "Lonesome."

Johnny Carroll and the Hot Rocks: "Rock Baby Rock It," "Wild Wild Women," "Crazy Crazy Love," "Rockin' Matbelle."

Don Coats and the Bon-Aires: "Love Never Forgets" and "China Star."

Cell Block 7: "The Saints Come Rockin' In" and "Hot Rock."

Rosco Gordon and the Red Tops: "Chicken in the Rough" and "Bop It."

The Five Stars: "Your Love Is All I Need" and "Hey Juanita."

Preacher Smith and the Deacons: "Eat Your Heart Out" and "Roogie Doogie."

All of the songs are available on a recently released Rhino soundtrack album.

The Reception

"Just what the teenagers want. Did top time business on a two-day change."—Charlie C. Webb, an Alabama exhibitor.

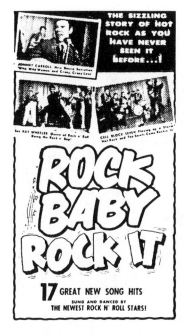

Top, left: Ad for *Rock Baby Rock It*. Top, right: Johnny Carroll. Bottom: The Cell Block Seven in *Rock Baby Rock It*.

The Five Stars in *Rock Baby Rock It*.

The Cast

Johnny Dobbs, Kay Wheeler, Joan Arnold, Bill Brookshire, Gayla Graves, Mike Biggs, Linda Moore, Lee Young, David Miller.

The Credits

Director Murray Douglas Sporup, *Producer* J.G. Tiger, *Director of Photography* Henry Kokojan, *Editor* Barton Hayes, *Sound* Howard Greeve. B&W.

Sources

Boxoffice, Vol. 71, No. 14, July 27, 1957, pg. 12; Clark, *Rock and Roll in the Movies*. No. 1.

Rock 'n' Roll Revue

This "revue" was presented like a stage show and probably released around 1956. Musical interludes, quelled from a series called

Ad for **Rock 'n' Roll Jamboree,** which became **Rock 'n' Roll Revue.**

"Telescription," are spliced together with newly filmed comedy bits supplied by Mantan Moreland. It's a who's who in rhythm and blues.

Ruth Brown, dubbed Miss Rhythm, sings "Tears Come Tumbling Down." Born January 30, 1928, in Virginia, she sang in USOs during World War II and later with Lucky Millinder's band until Cab Calloway's sister Blanche took her to Atlantic records. Jerry Leiber and

Mike Stoller wrote her a song, "Lucky Lips," that took her out of the rhythm and blues charts and onto the pop charts. "Please Don't Freeze" was a personal favorite of music critic Bobette Milici. Ruth still sings at jazz festivals now and then.

Harold Lucas, Matthew McQuarter, John Bailey, Harold Winley, and Bill Harris, collectively known as The Clovers, sing "Your Cash Ain't Nothing But Trash," available on Atlantic. Leiber and Stoller placed them on the pop charts too, in 1959, with a song called "Love Potion No. 9." Their 1956 R&B hit, "Devil or Angel," became a bigger hit for Bobby Vee years later. The Clovers are considered one of the first rock groups.

The incomparable Nat "King" Cole sings "The Trouble with You Is Me." Cole never had any trouble placing records on the pop charts because he sounded more white than white singers. His sound was smooth and gentle and it seemed during the forties and fifties no matter what he sang it sold—"Mona Lisa," "Too Young," "Pretend"—the list of titles would fill the page. Yet, in spite of his popularity with white audiences, he often wasn't allowed to stay in the hotels where he was welcomed as a performer. When Cole wanted to buy a home in Beverly Hills a special meeting was called to see what could be done to keep him out. Cole showed up and told the group "I was thinking about buying a home here but I heard there was an undesirable moving into the neighborhood and I wanted to find out more about it." He died in 1965 from lung cancer. His daughter, Natalie, is a hit-maker herself.

Dinah Washington had her biggest hit in 1959—"What a Difference a Day Makes"—but she also has a long list of R&B hits. She was born in Alabama on August 29, 1924, and less than 20 years later was singing the blues with Lionel Hampton, who is also featured in this film. She died from an overdose of sleeping pills in 1963 shortly after her seventh marriage to Dick "Night Train" Lane of the Detroit Lions.

The Music

Ruth Brown: "Tears Come Tumbling Down," available on Atlantic.

The Clovers: "Your Cash Ain't Nothing But Trash," available on Atlantic.

Nat Cole: "The Trouble with You Is Me," available on Capitol.

Larry Darnell: "What More Do You Want Me to Do?"

Delta Rhythm Boys: "Take the 'A' Train."

Duke Ellington: "The Mooch."
Martha Davis: "Vip-i-ty Vip-i-ty Vop."
Lionel Hampton: "Beulah's Boogie."
Joe Turner: "Oke-she-moke-she-pop."
Dinah Washington: "Only a Moment Ago."

The Cast

Willie Bryant (m.c.), Coles and Atkins (tap dancers), Little Buck (tap dancer), "Nipsy" Russell, Mantan Moreland.

The Credits

Studio Films, Inc. Color 72 min.

Sources

Nite, *Rock On.*

Rock Pretty Baby! (1956)

This film attempted to capture a broader audience by eliminating the so-called offensive elements normally associated with rock movies — delinquent behavior, sloppy dress, contempt for authority, drag races, etc. While some adults may have found comfort in this approach, it is unlikely that even they enjoyed the results. The movie is afraid to rock or roll and is less entertaining than any given episode of *Leave It to Beaver.*

Although Sal Mineo gets top billing, the film really belongs to John Saxon, who made his screen debut the previous year in Universal-International's *Running Wild,* followed by a meatier role as a disturbed youth in the same studio's *The Unguarded Moment.* Audience response to the actor in the latter film caused the studio to do a last-minute revamp in their campaign for this film to take advantage of Saxon's rising popularity. He played the leader of a high school rock band at odds with his doctor daddy (Ed Platt) who wants him to give up music for medicine.

"I have a scene with Ed Platt where we have an argument and I trashed a guitar," recalled Saxon. "The director, Dick Bartlett, was very sincere about all of us doing a good job so I really got into this moment.

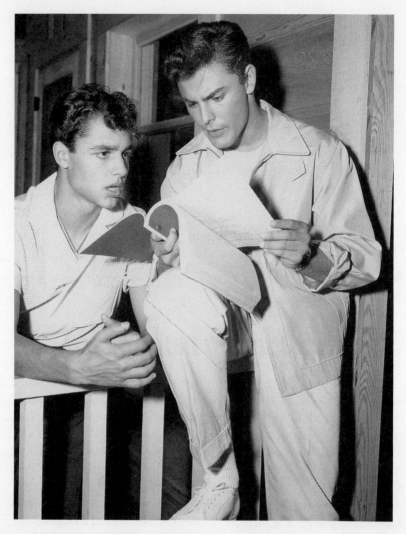

**Sal Mineo (left) and John Saxon rehearse a scene from *Rock Pretty Baby!*
originally titled *Crazy Love*.**

After we did the scene I heard one of the grips say, 'If I had a kid like
that I'd kill him.' So I guess I did okay."

Papa redeems himself in the end by breaking several traffic laws
to get Saxon to a band contest on time. The band loses, but they get a
two-week gig at a summer camp anyway, which is where the sequel,
Summer Love, picks up.

Nobody in Saxon's band, including Saxon, actually performs the music the band is shown playing, though no credit is given to the people who ghosted for them. There are six songs and at least as many instrumentals, but the instrumentals are so similar (written by Henry Mancini) it is difficult to give an accurate account. Even the studio's publicity department couldn't seem to decide, their estimates ranging between twelve and eighteen, depending on which press release you happen to read.

Henry Mancini was born in Cleveland, Ohio, on April 16, 1924, and grew up in Pennsylvania, where he studied piano. After high school he went to New York, where he attended the Julliard school of music. After three years in the military he joined the Glenn Miller Band and married Ginny O'Connor. Jerry Gray, the band's arranger, helped him get a job at Universal writing music for the studio's stock music library. Mancini was with the studio from 1952 to 1958 and received no credit for the bulk of his work. U-I alumnus Blake Edwards asked him to compose music for Edwards' TV series *Peter Gunn*, which netted the composer two Grammies and made him one of the best-known soundtrack artists ever. Many of his themes became hit records, most notably "Moon River" from *Breakfast at Tiffany's* (1961), for which he won an Oscar; "Baby Elephant Walk" from *Hatari* (1962); the song from *Days of Wine and Roses* (1962), another Oscar winner; and the theme from *The Pink Panther* (1964). But rock and roll wasn't Mancini's forte, and his music for *Rock Pretty Baby!* is easily his worst.

Reaction to the film when it was previewed at the Academy Theatre in Pasadena, California, was so favorable U-I decided to try something it had never done before. At another sneak, this time in Encino, they got the audience reaction on film instead of preview cards. Sal Mineo was sent to Florida for the premiere there and hundreds of fans that gathered for autographs caused a major traffic problem. In Washburn, South Dakota, the picture was booked during the city's Diamond Jubilee, a three-day carnival which was expected to keep the theatre empty. Instead it did the best business that year.

The Music

Jimmy Daley and His Ding-A-Lings (actual performers unknown): "Rock Pretty Baby," "What's It Gonna Be," "Rockabye Lullabye Blues," and "Can I Steal a Little Love," available on a Decca soundtrack album

(Left–right) Rod McKuen, John Saxon, and April Kent in *Rock Pretty Baby!*

which recently resurfaced on MCA. "What's It Gonna Be" was also released on Capitol by The Four Freshmen. "Can I Steal a Little Love" was on Capitol as well, sung by Frank Sinatra.

Henry Mancini: "Hot Rod," "Big Band Rock 'N' Roll," "Rockin' the Boogie," "Juke Box Rock," "Teen Age Bop," "Dark Blue," "Kool Kid," "The Most," "Young Love," and "Free and Easy," all part of the Decca soundtrack.

Rod McKuen: "Picnic by the Sea" and "Happy Is a Boy Named Me" on the soundtrack album. A single by Joan Hager of the latter song, retitled "Happy Is a Girl Named Me" was released on Decca. Album currently available on Epic.

The Reception

". . . must be judged for the purpose it was made — to cash in on the rock and roll frenzy. Considered from any other standpoint, the picture is dull and embarrassing. It'll make adults squirm and probably drive them out of the theatres." — *Motion Picture Daily*.

"This is a fine picture for the entire family. A good story and a good show. Drew very well to a profit. Nuff sed."—W.L. Stratton, an exhibitor in Challis, Idaho.

"The swing away from the juvenile delinquency angle is a refreshing twist that the teenagers should like, just as they will the celluloid dealings with normal growing up problems. While there's plenty of rock and roll music in the footage, the title is still not too indicative of content and may sidetrack prospective adult patrons."—*Variety*.

"Seems this is what the teenagers and younger ones want. This was our fourth rock and roll show in April, so it did not do an outstanding business for that reason. Wish we could see more of them in color."—Mickey and Penny Harris, New Boston, Texas, exhibitors.

". . . stretches into the longest hour and a half in recent movie history."—*The Los Angeles Times*.

"Although no door buster by the time I got around to it, it did please those who came, including yours truly."—I. Roche, an exhibitor in Vernon, Florida.

"It is a well-paced story of problems and situations easily identifiable by those in their teens and early twenties, a tasteful but explicit romance, some small scale but zestful musical interludes and a good family comedy."—*The Hollywood Reporter*.

"Oh, yes, they came, they saw, they liked every minute of it. A really good story, also. Play it. You can make dough off it if bought middle bracket."—Sam Holmberg, an exhibitor in Sturgis, Saskatchewan.

"It's in B-W, which is against it and the cast is very little known. Not a bad picture, but Easter exams kept the young folks away and the oldsters did not seem to want to see it. . . . Rock and roll pictures on the way out here."—F.L. Murray, Spiritwood, Saskatchewan.

"We had a 97 per cent teenage trade but enough to make it the best in nine months here at the Roxy. Don't call it rock 'n' roll music. Boy, it is happiness music for a small town theatre. I love those teenage moviegoers. Oh, yes, it is a good family-type pleasing picture."—Ken Christianson, an exhibitor in Washburn, South Dakota.

"Our teenagers really went for this one and we're looking forward to bringing it back in the near future. . . . Adults might like some of the parts, since there are some misunderstanding parents in it."—Jerry Walden, exhibitor in Seagoville, Texas.

The Cast

Sal Mineo (Nino Barrato), John Saxon (Jimmy Daley), Luana Patten (Joan Wright), Edward C. Platt (Dr. Thomas Daley), Fay Wray (Beth Daley), Rod McKuen ("Ox" Bentley), John Wilder ("Fingers" Porter), Alan Reed, Jr. ("Sax" Lewis), Bob Courtney ("Half-Note" Harris), Douglas Fowley ("Pop" Wright), George Winslow (Thomas Daley, III), Johnny Grant (himself), April Kent (Kay Norton), Sue George (Lori Parker), Susan Volkmann (Carol Saunders), Caryl Volkmann (Claire Saunders), Shelley Fabares (Teressa "Twinky" Daley), Glen Kramer (Bruce Carter).

The Credits

Director Richard Bartlett, *Producer* Edmond Chevie, *Screenplay* Herbert Margolis and William Raynor, *Director of Photography* George Robinson, A.S.C., *Art Directors* Alexander Golitzen and Philip Barber, *Set Decorators* Russell A. Gausman and Ruby R. Levitt, *Editor* Frederick Y. Smith, A.C.E., *Assistant Director* Ronnie Rondell, *Music* Henry Mancini. B&W 89 min. Universal-International.

Sources

Boxoffice, Vol. 70, No. 24, April 6, 1957, pg. 12; Vol. 70, No. 25, April 13, 1957, pg. 12; Vol. 71, No. 4, May 18, 1957, pg. 12; Vol. 71, No. 9, June 27, 1957, pg. 12; Vol. 71, No. 16, August 10, 1957, pg. 12; Vol. 73, No. 4, May 19, 1958, pg. 14; Bronson, *Billboard Book of Number One Hits*.

Rock, Rock, Rock (1956)

This extremely low budget genre entry was shot in nine days in a little place in the Bronx called the Bedford Park Studios (though one of the producers said it was a misnomer to call the place a studio). Many of the exteriors were shot at the botanical gardens near the studio, photographed by Morris Hartzband, a veteran of TV's "Naked City" series. The Distributors Corporation of America (DCA) financed it, and producers Max Rosenberg and Milton Subotsky were canny enough to

Ad for *Rock, Rock, Rock*.

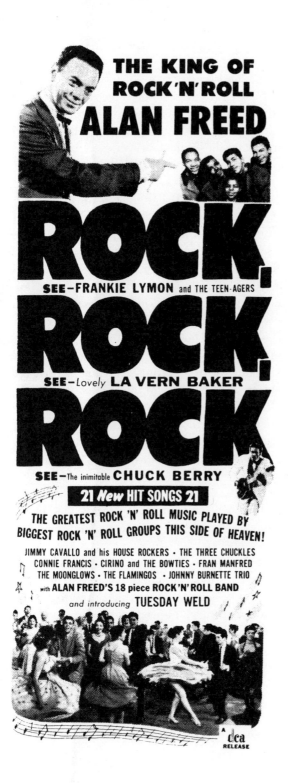

sign disc jockey Alan Freed to play a leading role. Although Rosenberg credited Paul Case with selecting the singers for the film, it is likely that Freed played a substantial role as many of the performers often appeared on Freed's legendary stage shows. At times this movie comes close to being one of those shows with Freed introducing one act after another, often five at a crack with no interference from the thin plot.

According to Freed he'd dabbled in music since he was a kid, although there's little evidence of it. He toyed with the idea of being a trombonist after a Cleveland Symphony Orchestra concert but never took lessons. In college he took mechanical engineering and journalism, the former for his father, the latter for himself. He hated engineering and was relieved when he was drafted into the Signal Corps, where double mastoiditis damaged his hearing. (Several unkind critics of rock music believed this accounted for his affection for the music.) After he was medically discharged he went back to college to finish his engineering degree and set his sights on becoming a disc jockey. He was told that his Midwest accent was too grating. Undaunted, Freed got a job as a sports announcer at WAKR in Akron, Ohio. "One night," Freed recalled, "as I finished the 11:10 sports broadcast, I got a very quick call saying the disc jockey for the 11:15 show had not shown up. As I was the only announcer in the studio, I was elected. I grabbed a stack of records, any records, and the engineer in the control room told me which ones were popular." The next day Freed got a call from the sponsor, who liked what he'd done. The other DJ was fired and Freed got the job. In 1953 he moved to Cleveland, and at WJW he called himself Moon Dog House on a show called "Record Rendezvous," which ultimately became "Rock 'N' Roll Party," a program that tailored black rhythm and blues for white audiences. By calling the music rock and roll Freed eliminated the racial stigma attached to it. Freed organized an ill-fated rock show in the Cleveland Arena which drew over 25,000 kids to a 10,000-seat stadium. A riot broke out that made the national news. Five people were arrested and one person was knifed. And so the seed was planted: Rock and roll led to violence. (No one seemed to remember that back in 1938 there were similar riots during Benny Goodman's performances.) There was another outbreak of violence during one of Freed's shows in Boston. The police refused to allow the arena lights to be dimmed during the performance, and Freed told his audience, "I guess the police here in Boston don't want you kids to have a good time!"

Top: Alan Freed. Bottom: Frankie Lymon and the Teenagers. From *Rock, Rock, Rock.*

It ended with fifteen persons stabbed, slugged, beaten or robbed. A dozen police cars rushed in to restore order. But in spite of the trouble, Freed continued to serve as one of the leading spokesmen for rock music, the "high lama of rock 'n' roll," as one writer called him. While other DJs played white versions of black songs, Freed staunchly stuck to the originals. Most of the performers in *Rock, Rock, Rock* are black.

The Music

The Flamingos sing "Would I Be Crying" in the film. A doo-wop group from Chicago, the Flamingos had their first national hit the year of *Rock, Rock, Rock,* "I'll Be Home." The group was formed in 1952 and consisted of Nathaniel Nelson (born April 10, 1932), John Carter, Ezekiel Carey (born January 24, 1933), Paul Wilson (born January 6, 1935), Jacob Carey (born September 9, 1926), and Sollie McElroy. (Another source lists Earl Lewis as part of the original lineup.) In 1956 Carter and Zeke Carey were drafted into the army and were replaced by Tommy Hunt (born June 18, 1933) and Terry Johnson (born November 12, 1935). The group signed with Decca the following year and scored a hit with a song called "Ladder of Love." Their biggest hit was "I Only Have Eyes for You" in 1959.

Frankie Lymon and the Teenagers was a group that began singing on street corners of Harlem in 1954, all school buddies. There were Sherman Garnes (born June 8, 1940), Joe Negroni (born September 9, 1940), Herman Santiago (born February 18, 1941), Jimmy Merchant (born February 10, 1940) and, of course, Lymon (born September 30, 1942). Richard Barrett, the lead of a group called the Valentines, heard them and introduced them to George Goldner and Joe Kilsky at Gee records. Goldner and Kilsky were crazy about one of the songs that young Lymon had written, "Why Do Fools Fall in Love," which became their first hit record, despite the cover versions by Gale Storm and The Diamonds. Legend has it that Santiago was supposed to sing the lead on the song, but he had a bad throat that afternoon and Lymon stepped in. Shortly after their appearance in *Rock, Rock, Rock* Lymon left the group for a solo career and had a hit record, "Goody Goody," before his voice changed. After that he turned to drugs, for which he was arrested ten years later. One of the national magazines reported that he kicked the habit, but when his attempted comeback at eighteen failed he got hooked again. A girlfriend kept him clean for a year, but when they broke up and Lymon entered the army, he slipped back. He died in 1968 from an overdose of heroine in his grandmother's apartment. Sherman Garnes died during open heart surgery in 1977; Joe Negroni died the following year of an aneurysm of the brain. Jimmy Merchant, Herman Santiago and a woman who sounds like Lymon, Pearl McKinnon, still perform as Frankie Lymon's Teenagers.

The Moonglows had appeared in a number of Alan Freed's stage shows prior to their performance in *Rock, Rock, Rock.* Freed had been instrumental in their success by getting them their first two recording contracts, first with Champagne and after that company folded with Chance. Freed also helped himself by taking writing credit for many of their songs. Once billed as Bobby Lester and the Moonglows, the original members of the group were Lester (born January 13, 1930), Pete Graves (born April 17, 1936), Prentiss Barnes (born 1921), Billy Johnson (born 1924), and Harvey Fuqua (born 1924).* Fuqua eventually took over as lead singer, and in 1958 the group had its biggest hit ever, "Ten Commandments of Love," released under the name Harvey and the Moonglows, after which the group disbanded. Fuqua (whose uncle was Charley Fuqua, one of the original Ink Spots) continued to record with Chess, had his own record labels (Harvey Records and Tri Phi Records) and had a major hit with a song called "That's What Girls Are Made For," backed by a group called The Spinners (with Marvin Gaye as one of its members). Fuqua married Berry Gordy's sister and became a producer at Gordy's Motown Records in the mid–1960s. Bobby Lester died of cancer in 1980 at his home in Louisville, Kentucky.

Once known as "Little Miss Sharecropper," La Vern Baker had had a few hit records on the R&B charts—"Tweedlee Dee," "Bop-Ting-A-Ling" and "Play It Fair"—before she stepped in front of the camera to appear in Rosenberg's and Subotsky's movie and was a regular in Alan Freed's stage shows. But her biggest hit, "Jim Dandy," hit the charts shortly after the release of this film. Born in Chicago on November 11, 1929, she had contracts with Columbia and King before Ahmet Ertegun and Herb Abramson signed her at Atlantic, where she recorded her most successful records. Her record sales were repeatedly hampered by white cover versions, so much so that she wrote a letter of complaint to her Detroit congressman. Following her biggest pop hit, "I Cried a

*One source lists Prentis Graves, Alexander Graves, and Buddy Johnson.

LaVern Baker performs in *Rock, Rock, Rock*.

Tear," her career began sagging and after her move to Japan she stopped singing in the United States.

Johnny Burnette, one of the few white singers in *Rock, Rock, Rock*, was a rockabilly pioneer. His trio consisted of himself, his friend Paul Burlison, and his brother Dorsey. They were working as electricians in Memphis for the same company that had once employed Elvis Presley as a truck driver when they won a Ted Mack talent contest which led to a recording contract with Coral. The trio broke up around 1958, after the Burnette brothers had written several hits for Ricky Nelson. Dorsey signed with Era and had two hits, "Tall Oak Tree" and "Hey Little One." Johnny had his first national hit in 1960, "Dreamin'" followed by "You're Sixteen," both for Liberty. (Years later ex–Beatle Ringo Starr had a hit with "You're Sixteen.") Johnny died in 1964, the victim of a fishing accident. His son Rocky had a hit of his own in 1979, "Tired of Toein' the Line."

Another white singer, Teddy Randazzo, sings three numbers in *Rock, Rock, Rock*, although he's no rocker. Born May 20, 1937, in New York, he began his career as one of the Chuckles with Tom Tomano and Russ Gilberto. Although he never scored big on the charts himself, he wrote several hits for Little Anthony and the Imperials, including "Goin' Out of My Head," which was also a smash for The Lettermen years later. All of these singers (and many more) are sandwiched between poorly staged vignettes of Tuesday Weld's efforts to get enough money to buy a new dress for the senior prom. The fact that it never crosses her mind to work for the money makes Weld's character unintentionally unsympathetic. Instead she tries to pry it out of her father, who's already given the little twit more than she deserves. When he refuses she goes to the bank. She's turned down but comes away with a plan: If the bank can make money by charging 3 percent on a loan, she'll make money by taking some of their business away at 1 percent interest. She borrows fifteen bucks from her best friend and loans it to an even bigger twit, believing that 1 percent of fifteen bucks is fifteen bucks. When her boyfriend hears that she's charging 100 percent interest it causes a riff between them until he realizes she's not a crook, she's just stupid.

"Tuesday Weld was a lovely young lady to work with," said producer Max Rosenberg. "Sweet and gentle and lovely. All in all it was a very nice picture."

Miss Weld has a couple of numbers to sing herself, her voice dubbed by Connie Francis, whose career hadn't quite taken off yet. Born Constance Franconero on December 12, 1938, in New Jersey, Connie Francis was performing professionally at the age of eleven. Shortly after this picture her domineering father suggested she record an old standard, "Who's Sorry Now" (later the title of her autobiography), which became a million-seller. A rapid succession of hits followed, including the title track from her first major motion picture, *Where the Boys Are* (1960). Her film career was short-lived and by the mid–1960s her days as a number one hit maker had come to an end. An attack by a rapist in 1974 pretty much ended her career altogether as the experience was so traumatic it caused the loss of her voice for several years.

Moe Waxman, the manager of a theatre in Philadelphia, got the surprise of his life when he ran *Rock, Rock, Rock*. His patrons (and not all of them in their teens) began clapping and stomping to the music. Nearly 400 people started dancing in the aisles and in the lobby. Afraid that things would get out of hand, Waxman placed a frantic call to the police. Thirty policemen, eight patrol cars, and two patrol wagons later the enthusiastic dancers were cleared from the theatre, some of them

Chuck Berry performed "You Can't Catch Me" in *Rock, Rock, Rock*.

dancing all the way into the street while the rest of the audience kept their seats and the rhythm. No one was hurt. Bob Kessler, another Philadelphia exhibitor, got the message and staged a dance marathon in connection with the picture. Movies were shot and run the following week at the various establishments that donated prizes to the winners.

When Alan Freed was asked to appear on Mike Wallace's TV show he declined. "Why argue about rock 'n' roll," he told Wallace. "It's bigger than both of us."

La Vern Baker: "Tra-La-La," available on Atlantic.

Chuck Berry: "You Can't Catch Me," available on Chess.

The Johnny Burnette Trio: "Lonesome Train," which may have been released on Coral.

Jimmy Cavallo and His House Rockers: "The Big Beat" and "Rock, Rock, Rock."

Cirino and the Bowties: "Ever Since I Can Remember."

The Flamingos: "Would I Be Crying?" available on Chess.

Connie Francis: "Little Blue Wren" and "That's Never Happened to Me."

Frankie Lymon and the Teenagers: "I'm Not a Juvenile Delinquent" and "Baby Baby," available on the LP "Why Do Fools Fall in Love" on Gee.

The Moonglows: "I Knew from the Start" and "Over and Over Again," available on Chess.

Teddy Randazzo: "We're Gonna Rock Tonight," "You'll Have the Things Your Heart Needs," "Thanks to You," and "Won't You Give Me a Chance."

Al Sears: "Right Now."

Ivy Schulman: "Baby Wants to Rock."

NOTE: Chess has recently reissued a soundtrack album from the film with the following songs from the film: "Over and Over Again," "I Knew from the Start," "You Can't Catch Me," "Would I Be Crying," plus material not in the film: "Sincerely" and "See Saw" by the Moonglows, "Maybellene," "Roll Over Beethoven," and "Thirty Days" by Chuck Berry, "I'll Be Home," "A Kiss from Your Lips," and "The Vow" by the Flamingos.

The Reception

"The film, about an hour and a half in length, has all the earmarks of a rush job to cash in on the rock and roll craze among adolescents." — *Hollywood Citizens News.*

"It outgrossed so many of the big supers that it amazed even me. It paid the overhead and made a few bucks besides and darned if I don't think I'll repeat it soon." — Victor Webber, an exhibitor in Arkansas.

"Serious students of contemporary juvenile musical phenomena can have themselves a ball trying to figure out what makes the kids rock and the back roll in this latest example of the rock and roll craze. . . . The twitchy epic cost $125,000 to make (which is peanuts in filmmaking) and is expected to gross well over a million." — *Cue.*

"This did excellent business. Of course, mostly teenagers but the picture is a little 'hammy' or at least, that's my personal opinion. Not nearly as good as *Shake, Rattle and Rock,* but why should I complain, with it doing very fine business and pleasing the ones it was intended to please. Fact is, I could use more like it." — Anonymous Alabama exhibitor.

"It has the look of a pasted-together quickie aimed only at some fast b.o. cash. . . . There's even a phony applause track thrown in, a la many TV shows." — *Boxoffice.*

"This is just music, not much of a story. Brought out the teenagers in droves, so business was good but 'no comment' on the picture." — Harold Smith, an exhibitor in Iowa.

"The makers have assembled an unimpressive display of rock and roll talent, very few of the acts displaying anything worthwhile." — *Variety.*

"Here's a swell show from a small company. We had it on a single bill plus a rock and roll contest, and business was fine. This one should do the same anywhere." — A. Madril, an exhibitor in Colorado.

The Cast

Alan Freed (himself), Fran Manfred (Arabella), Tuesday Weld (Dori Grey), Connie Francis (singing voice of Dori Grey), Teddy Randazzo (Tommy Baker), Jacqueline Kerr (Gloria), Ivy Schulman (Baby), Jack Collins (Mr. Grey), Carol Moss (Mrs. Grey), Eleanor Swayne (Miss Silky), Lester Mack (Mr. Bimble), Bert Conway (Mr. Baker), David Winters (Melville), The Moonglows (themselves), Chuck Berry (himself), The Flamingos (themselves), Jimmy Cavallo and His House Rockers (themselves), The Johnny Burnette Trio (themselves), La Vern Baker (herself), Cirino and the Bowties (themselves), Frankie Lymon and the Teenagers (themselves), and The Coney Island Kids (themselves).

The Credits

Director Will Price, *Producer* Max J. Rosenberg and Milton Subotsky, *Screenplay* Milton Subotsky, *Story* Milton Subotsky and Phyllis Coe, *Director of Photography* Morris Hartzband, *Editor* Blandine Hafeia, *Musical Director* Milton Subotsky, *Sound* William J. Schwartz. B&W 83 min. Vanguard/DCA.

Sources

Boxoffice, Vol. 70, No. 16, February 9, 1957, pgs. 12 and 32; Vol. 70, No. 24, April 6, 1957, pg. 12; Herman, *Rock 'N' Roll Babylon;* Miller, *Rolling Stone History of Rock & Roll;* Nite, *Rock On;* Pareles and Romanowski, *Rolling Stone Encyclopedia of Rock & Roll;* Stambler, *Encyclopedia of Pop Rock and Soul.*

Rumble on the Docks (1956)

Here was another look at the battle between business and labor unions which Columbia routinely made to take advantage of their own *On the Waterfront.* In his film debut James Darren is the leader of a street gang who perjures himself to help a gangster he admires. The gangster goes gunning for Darren just to make certain the boy doesn't have a change of mind.

This was made to support *Don't Knock the Rock,* but it is in no way a rock movie except for the appearance of Freddie Bell and his Bellboys, a group featured in *Rock Around the Clock.*

The Music

Freddie Bell and His Bellboys: "Rumble on the Docks" and "Take the First Train Out of Town."

The Reception

". . . better than average low-budget picture despite a somewhat questionable premise, that gang wars between young hoodlums in the Brooklyn dock are all right as long as the young men use nothing more lethal than their fists." — *Hollywood Reporter.*

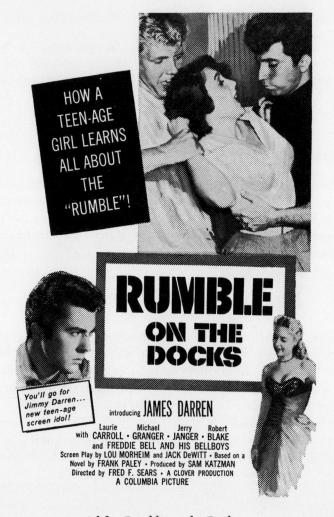

HOW A
TEEN-AGE
GIRL LEARNS
ALL ABOUT
THE
"RUMBLE"!

RUMBLE
ON THE
DOCKS

You'll go for
Jimmy Darren...
new teen-age
screen idol!

introducing JAMES DARREN

Laurie   Michael   Jerry   Robert
with CARROLL • GRANGER • JANGER • BLAKE
and FREDDIE BELL AND HIS BELLBOYS
Screen Play by LOU MORHEIM and JACK DeWITT • Based on a
Novel by FRANK PALEY • Produced by SAM KATZMAN
Directed by FRED F. SEARS • A CLOVER PRODUCTION
A COLUMBIA PICTURE

Ad for *Rumble on the Docks.*

"... gutsy Sam Katzman production. ... Film packs considerable
violence, but get in good characterizations and is an okay entry for action houses."— *Variety.*

The Cast

James Darren (Jimmy Smigelski), Laurie Carroll (Della), Michael
Granger (Joe Brindo), Jerry Janger (Rocky), Robert Blake (Chuck),

Edgar Barrier (Pete Smigelski), Celia Lovsky (Anna Smigelski), David Bond (Dan Kevlin), Timothy Carey (Frank Mangus), Dan Terranova (Tony Lightning), Barry Froner (Poochie), Don Devlin (Wimpie), Stephen H. Sears (Cliffie), Joseph Vitale (Ferdinand Marchesi), David Orrick (Gotham), Larry Blake (Fitz), Robert C. Ross (Gil Danco), Steve Warren (Sully), Don Garrett (Bo-Bo), Josel Ashley (Fuller), Salvatore Anthony (14-year-old).

The Credits

Director Fred F. Sears, *Producer* Sam Katzman, *Screenplay* Lou Morheim and Jack DeWitt from the novel by Frank Paley, *Director of Photography* Benjamin H. Kline, A.S.C., *Assistant Director* Willard Sheldon, *Art Director* Paul Palmentola, *Editor* Jerome Thoms, A.C.E., *Music* Mischa Bakaleinikoff. B&W 84 min. A Clover Production. Columbia Pictures.

Shake, Rattle and Rock! (1956)

Shake was the first movie produced by the newly formed American International Pictures aimed at the juvenile trade. It proved to be so successful the company continued to make movies almost exclusively for the teenage market — and took a lot of heat for doing it from the sort of folks depicted in this film. The screenplay is a rehash of Sam Katzman's *Don't Knock the Rock* (1956), written by Lou Rusoff, brother-in-law of Sam Arkoff, one of the co-founders of AIP. In Katzman's film a rock singer battled the citizens of his hometown when they wanted to ban rock music. It's a TV dance show host in Rusoff's scenario who ultimately convinces the irate citizens that rock music is no more dangerous than the jazz music of their youth.

The big attraction of this film is Fats Domino, who has three numbers,* one of them the classic "Ain't That a Shame." His sequences were shot months ahead of the rest of the production to accommodate Domino's busy schedule, which is why he's never actually shown with any of the characters in the story. He was paid $1,500, which wasn't bad for a day's work.

*Your author only saw two numbers but as it was on TV "Honey Chile" may have been cut for time.

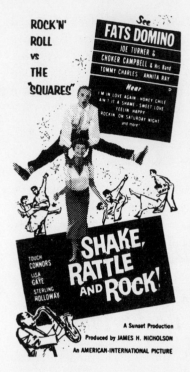

Left: Ad for *Shake, Rattle and Rock!* Right: Fats Domino.

Born Antoine Domino on either February 26, 1928, or May 10, 1929, in New Orleans, he was the only one of nine children who took to music. He started playing piano when he was eight, hammering away at the old upright that belonged to one of his cousins. His brother-in-law Harrison Verrett taught him how to play it. At 14 Domino quit school and went to work in a mattress factory so he could play clubs at night. His hands were crushed in an accident at the factory and it looked as if his piano playing days were over, but that obviously wasn't the case. At 20 he cut his first record, "The Fat Man," for Lew Chudd's Imperial Records. It sold 800,000 copies during its first year; a million by the second. Chudd had seen Domino at a little place called the Hideaway Bar, where he was earning three bucks a week with Dave Bartholomew's dance band playing a form of boogie-woogie called jump-blues. Chudd signed Domino and Bartholomew on the spot, and in their early days with Imperial both men cut records independently of each other. Then "Ain't That a Shame" (or "Ain't It a Shame") crossed the color barrier.

Top: Fats Domino at the keyboard. Bottom: Joe Turner smiles for the camera. From *Shake, Rattle and Rock!*

Domino was thrust into the spotlight, and Bartholomew slipped quietly into the background as co-writer and arranger. Domino couldn't read or write music, so he'd sing his songs into a recorder for Bartholomew to transcribe. In 1954, following a string of hits, Domino was introduced to a crowd at the Annual Jazz Festival at Wrigley Field by Louis Armstrong as a man "deserving of membership in the Hall of Fame." Domino was headlining a little club in Ontario, California, when producer Alex Gordon asked him to appear in *Shake, Rattle and Rock!* Domino told him he had a free day in a couple of weeks. The two men agreed that Gordon would pick Domino up at the Roosevelt Hotel and drive him to the studio.

A few days before the camera was set to roll Lew Chudd telephoned Gordon to say that Domino wouldn't appear in the film after all. He'd just signed a contract with 20th Century–Fox for $25,000 to sing one song in *Do Re Mi* (*The Girl Can't Help It,* 1956). Sam Arkoff got on the phone and told Chudd he'd get a restraining order unless Chudd agreed to honor their contract. The deal was back on.

A few days later Gordon blanched when the clerk at the Roosevelt Hotel told him Domino wasn't registered there. The movie had already been sold to the exhibitors, and with Domino's busy schedule Gordon was afraid there wouldn't be another chance. The clerk suggested he try the "other" Roosevelt Hotel, the one in the black section of Los Angeles. There Gordon encountered two burly bodyguards, who were grimly determined to let Fats get his sleep. Gordon desperately pushed his way past them and ran up the stairs to the singer's room. There he found Domino asleep and spent a few anxious moments when Domino couldn't remember what Gordon was talking about.

Joe Turner, often called "Big Joe" because of his 6'2", 250-pound frame, also appears in the film. Born Joseph Vernon Turner in Kansas City, Missouri (May 18, 1911), he doubled as a singer and a bouncer in the speakeasies he played in his youth. As a child he sold newspapers and junk to stay alive. He didn't get a break until 1938, when he played on a program with Benny Goodman in New York; but the folks didn't like his brand of blues, and Turner was back at the Apollo Theatre in Harlem when Ahmet Ertegun, the owner of Atlantic Records, signed him in 1951. His "Shake, Rattle and Roll" crossed over the black barrier and he's never had a bigger hit since.

Shake, Rattle and Rock! was completed in ten days by director Edward Cahn, an expert in fast-schedule pictures. Born February 12, 1899,

Top: Tommy Charles. Bottom: Either some lively dancing, or someone dropped a girl on this guy's head. From *Shake, Rattle and Rock!*

in Brooklyn, New York, Cahn entered films as a cutter at Universal and directed films for RKO, Fox and MGM during the 1940s, but by the 1950s he was linked exclusively with companies like AIP, United Artists and Columbia, cranking out potboilers until his death in 1963.

To help promote the picture, AIP sent a special exploitation package to disc jockeys across the country which contained records of the songs featured in the movie, stills for give-aways, and contest details.

"We played this with *Runaway Daughters* and drew our biggest Sunday and Monday crowd of the year," claimed O.M. Shannon in Portland, Texas. "If you book this when 'Fats' has a record on top, as we did, it cannot miss."

"This was my first picture from an independent company and I must say I like doing business with someone who isn't always begging me for play dates," said Harry Hawkinson, an exhibitor in Marietta, Minneapolis. "This is a wonderful rock and roll show. But I was very disappointed in business."

Harold Bell in Coaticook, Quebec, had the same problem but added, "We pleased a few youngsters with a very nice little picture, which should do more for others than it did for me." Which it did for S.T. Jackson in Alabama. "If you haven't used it you'd better do so pretty soon," Jackson urged. "It seems this is the type the people want to see these days." W.M. Finley in Arkansas happily reported that his customers "seemed to like this picture and we made some money clear on this one. Would recommend this picture to any theatre."

Although Alex Gordon actually produced the picture, AIP's president Jim Nicholson felt that it looked a little cheesy having Gordon's name on *Runaway Daughters* and *Shake, Rattle and Rock!* since both films were part of a package. Gordon's name was thus dropped from the credits and replaced with Nicholson's. It is curious that it didn't bother Nicholson to have director Cahn's and writer Lou Rusoff's names on both pictures.

The Music

Tommy Charles: "Sweet Love on My Mind."

Fats Domino: "I'm in Love Again," "Ain't That a Shame," and "Honey Chile," available on Imperial Records."

Anita Ray: "Rockin' on Saturday Night."

Joe Turner: "Feelin' Happy" and "Lipstick, Powder and Paint," the latter song released on the Atlantic label with "Rock a While" on the flip side.

The Reception

"A rather hasty little black and white pudding...." — *The Los Angeles Times.*
"For the rock and roll crowd this light entry should show good response." — *Variety.*
"There are some rock and roll artists involved whose names will aid in the marquee dressing and the picture itself is deftly enough done to please the younger fans." — *The Hollywood Reporter.*
"The film's conclusions . . . are arrived at in a singularly unpersuasive manner. . . . The numbers themselves . . . are surprisingly dull." — *Monthly Film Bulletin.*

The Cast

Fats Domino (himself), Joe Turner (himself), Lisa Gaye (June), Touch Connors (Garry Nelson), Sterling Holloway (Axe), Raymond Hatton (Horace), Douglas Dumbrille (Eustace Fentwick), Margaret Dumont (Georgianna), Tommy Charles (himself), Anita Ray (herself), Paul Dubov (Bugsy), Eddie Kafafian (Nick), Clarence Kolb (judge), Percy Helton (Hiram), Choker Campbell, Charles Evans (Bentley), Frank Jenks (director), Pierre Watkin (Armstrong), Joe Devlin (police captain), Jimmy Pickford (Eddie), Nancy Kilgas (Nancy), Giovanna Fiorino (Helen), Leon Tyler (Aloyisius), Patricia Gregory (Pat).

The Credits

Director Edward L. Cahn, *Producer* James H. Nicholson, *Story & Screenplay* Lou Rusoff, *Director of Photography* Frederick E. West, *Production Supervisor* Bart Carre, *Editor* Robert S. Eisen, *Art Director* Don Ament, *Music* Alexander Courage. A Sunset Production. B&W 78 min. An American International Picture.

Sources

Boxoffice, Vol. 71, No. 5, May 25, 1957, pg. 11; Vol. 71, No. 15, August 3, 1957, pg. 11; Vol. 71, No. 18, August 24, 1957, pg. 12; Vol. 71, No. 19, August 31, 1957, pg. 12; Miller, *Rolling Stone Illustrated History of Rock and Roll*; Stambler, *Encyclopedia of Pop Rock and Soul*.

Sing Boy Sing (1958)

This film was based on Paul Monash's "The Singing Idol," which was telecast on "Kraft Television Theatre" in January of 1957. The show presented a number of dramas concerning popular music with singers placed in dramatic roles (Gisele MacKenzie, Ferlin Husky, Julius La Rosa, Sal Mineo). Tommy Sands played the title role and introduced the song "Teenage Crush," which became a hit record. Sands reprises his role in the feature version, expanded by writer Claude Binyon to feature length. Sands used TV to promote the movie prior to its release.

Born August 27, 1937, in Chicago, Tommy Sands was singing at the age of nine and by twelve he was a disc jockey in Texas. "Teenage Crush" was his only hit although he continued to record on Capitol for several years after. With Annette Funicello he sang the title song of Walt Disney's *The Parent Trap* and together they appeared in Disney's *Babes in Toyland*. In the early sixties he married Nancy Sinatra and got a dramatic part in father Frank's *None But the Brave*. An unkind remark about Sands' appearance in the film from movie critic Kevin Thomas netted Thomas a punch in the nose from the actor, whose career ultimately suffered from bad publicity concerning his temper, his nervous breakdowns and a near fatal kidney ailment. After his divorce from Nancy, Sands married Sheila Wallace, moved to Hawaii, and continued to appear in nightclubs.

In *Sing Boy Sing* Sands played Virgil Walker, raised by his southern Bible-thumping grandpa and aunt. Grandpa wants the boy to be a preacher, but Sands is lured to the world of rock and roll music by a fast-talking and unscrupulous manager (played by Edmond O'Brien). The boy becomes famous, but he's lonely in tinsel town, and when his grandfather suffers a stroke, Virgil makes a death-bed promise to give up rock for religion. Virgil's aunt (Josephine Hutchinson) saves him from this horrible decision by convincing Virgil that God gave him his singing voice to make people happy.

The filmmakers were savvy enough to hire three of the nation's leading disc jockeys to appear in the film — Art Ford of New York, Bill Randle of Cleveland, and Biff Collie of Houston — giving the film built-in DJ support.

The Music

Tommy Sands: "Bundle of Dreams," "Crazy 'Cause I Love You," "I'm Gonna Walk and Talk with My Lord," "Just a Little Bit More," "People in Love," "Rock of Ages," "Sing Boy Sing," "Soda Pop Pop," "That's All I Want from You," "Your Daddy Wants to Do Right," "Who Baby," and "Would I Love You," released on a Capitol Soundtrack album and four EPs. "Sing Boy Sing" was released on a single.

The Reception

"Tommy Sands, said to be Elvis' chief competition in the realm of rock and roll, reveals considerable dramatic ability in his debut portrayal of a rural Louisiana teenager with voice who is discovered and created by a pair of sharp New York agents. . . . He sings much, much more clearly and grammatically than Elvis, is infinitely more wholesome and, with a few more

Ad for *Sing Boy Sing*.

Tommy Sands does what he's asked in *Sing Boy Sing.*

pictures to polish him, he's going to be a very competent actor . . . a welcome change." — *The Los Angeles Times.*

"A very enjoyable movie. Teenagers and children all came out, but mother and dad stayed home — I don't know why. It's worth playing anywhere." — R.W. Hollyoake, an exhibitor in Dauphin, Man.

"The first things the exhibitor wants to know about a new screen personality are, 'Does he look good and does he get across on film?' The answer is a big 'Yes!' . . . Tommy is not only a slim and vital juvenile but, what is more unexpected, he is a surprisingly sensitive and sincere young actor." — *Variety.*

"In my opinion, Sands is much better than Presley and he showed it in this." — James Hardy, an Indiana exhibitor.

"For the third time in roughly a year, 20th Century–Fox has come up with a screen debut of a hot juve vocal talent, in this case Tommy Sands. He registers as a potent new film personality who will, with proper material, become a box office lure of the calibre of Elvis Presley or Pat Boone." — *The Hollywood Reporter.*

"Not since we opened have we hit rock bottom like this. Even the teenagers called it square. They were being polite. I know the South African censors did quite a bit of cutting and re-editing for this one. . . . They should have saved everyone a lot of trouble and cut the rest of it, too."—Dave S. Klein, an exhibitor in Africa.

". . . the kind of movie to make any audience plain happy to have bought tickets. It has a strong, dramatic and contemporary story in which teenagers can identify themselves and their elders can watch with interest and compassion."—*The Los Angeles Examiner.*

"Did better than average business, but it did not do Presley business for me. Did well enough that I'm anxious for the next Tommy Sands pic."—S.T. Jackson, an exhibitor in Alabama.

"Rock and roll may be leaving but if *Sing Boy Sing* is any indication, Tommy Sands is coming like old 98 as an actor."—*Hollywood Citizens News.*

"If your patrons dig rock and roll, book this quick daddy-o, 'cause Tommy Sands is very big with hepsters."—*Film Daily.*

"Buddy Adler, whose recent smash hits starring Elvis Presley and Pat Boone proved him to be the ablest of Hollywood pied pipers, seems a cinch to rock the boxoffice and roll customers in the aisles with another sensation singing juvenile, Tommy Sands."—*Boxoffice.*

"A good picture, but too many had seen the story on TV. Really, boys, are stories so hard to find that you have to give us this? It did below average business for me, and Sands is, oh, so dead in Kensett."—Victor Weber, an exhibitor in Arkansas.

The Cast

Tommy Sands (Virgil Walker), Lili Gentle (Leora Easton), Edmond O'Brien (Joseph Sharkey), John McIntire (Rev. Walker), Nick Adams (C.K. Judd), Diane Jergens (Pat), Josephine Hutchinson (Caroline Walker), Jerry Paris (Fisher), Tami Conner (Ginnie), Regis Toomey (Rev. Easton), Art Ford (himself), Bill Randle (himself), Biff Collie (himself), Marie Brown (Mrs. Fitzgerald), Madge Cleveland (Miss Keyes), Tom Greenway (Haggerty), Lloyd Harter (Hillman), Patrick Miller (Fitzgerald).

The Credits

Producer-Director Henry Ephron, *Screenplay* Claude Binyon based on "The Singing Idol" teleplay by Paul Monash, *Assistant Director*

Hal Herman, *Director of Photography* William C. Mellor, A.S.C., *Art Directors* Lyle R. Wheeler and Herman A. Blumenthal, *Set* Walter M. Scott and Fay Babcock, *Editor* William Mace, *Sound* Eugene Grossman and Harold A. Root, *Music* Lionel Newman. C/S B&W 90 min. 20th Century–Fox.

Sources

Boxoffice, Vol. 72, No. 25, April 14, 1958, pg. 14; Vol. 74, No. 7, December 8, 1958, pg. 18; Vol. 74, No. 16, February 9, 1959, pg. 10; Vol. 75, No. 26, October 19, 1959, pg. 10; Brooks and Marsh, *Complete Directory to Prime Time Network TV Shows;* Katz, *Film Encyclopedia;* Ragan, *Who's Who in Hollywood.*

Summer Love (1958)

The adventures of Jimmy Daley and his combo, characters from Universal-International's *Rock Pretty Baby,* continue. This picture picks right up where the last one ended. Jimmy's group plays its two-week gig at a summer camp at Lake Arrowhead and finds time for romance between the rock and roll. The film was paired with *The Big Beat,* which gave the seekers of rock music a little more for their money.

The Music

According to the reviews this movie contains seven songs. "Summer Love" and "To Know You Is to Love You" were written by Bill Carey and Henry Mancini. Other songs include "Beatin' on the Bongos" and "Calypso Rock" and were penned by Rod McKuen, Malvina Reynolds, Everett Carter and Milton Rosen.

The Reception

"Although it is not as good as . . . earlier picture, it has some of the same stars. . . . Saxon has built a name in the interim, his draw, plus the goodwill created by the earlier picture . . . make this a profitable showing. . . ."—*Variety.*

"The high school set was pleased. Very few adults. I wouldn't give it much."—Frank E. Sabin, a Montana exhibitor.

"The adventure, romances, and tribulations of a five man rock and roll combo working on a country engagement has been made into a pleasing film with special appeal for the teenage audiences."—*Film Daily*.

"The first teenage picture since *Rock Pretty Baby* that has come through. I believe it was the magic of Molly Bee. Cute, clean, family entertainment, the best of its kind."—Ken Christianson, an exhibitor in North Dakota.

"This is a fine family and teenage picture with none of the rough stuff that one finds as a rule in pictures aimed at teenagers. Maybe it would have been better if it had had some rough spots in it for it did not do too well."—Victor Weber, an exhibitor in Arkansas.

"Director Haas must have had complete confidence in his script and his young players for he confidently uses his camera to go out on a background character he intends to use as the focal point in the following scene."—*Variety*.

The Cast

John Saxon (Jim Daley), Molly Bee (Alice), Rod McKuen ("Ox" Bentley), Judy Meredith (Joan Wright), Jill St. John (Erica Landis), John Wilder (Mike Howard), George Winslow (Thomas Daley, III), Fay Wray (Beth Daley), Edward C. Platt (Thomas Daley), Shelley Fabares (Twinkie Daley), Gordon Gebert (Tad Powers), Beverly Washburn (Jackie), Bob Courtney (Half-Note Harris), Troy Donahue (San Lewis), Hylton Socker (Fingers Porter), Marjorie Durant (Hilda), Walter Reed (Mr. Reid).

The Credits

Director Charles Haas, *Producer* William Grady, Jr., *Screenplay* William Raynor and Herbert Margolis, *Director of Photography* Carl E. Guthrie, *Editor* Tony Martinelli, *Music* Henry Mancini. B&W 85 min. Universal-International.

Sources

Boxoffice, Vol. 73, No. 7, June 8, 1958, pg. 6.

Untamed Youth (1957)

Originally titled *Flaming Youth*, this was sold to the public as another juvenile delinquency yarn with rock and roll music. In reality it was a movie about adult delinquents. Its makers were Aubrey Schenck and Howard W. Koch, who were very active in low-budget films during the 1950s. Schenck (born August 26, 1908) was a lawyer for a theater chain in the mid-thirties and switched to production a decade later. Koch (born April 11, 1916) was a film cutter at Fox who graduated to second unit directing and ultimately became vice president in charge of production at Paramount in the mid-sixties. Together they formed Bel Air Productions and made a number of potboilers, usually for United Artists. *Untamed Youth* was released by Warner Bros. It may not have been much of a teenage film but as a lurid, sleazy melodrama it ranked with the best of them.

Plantation owner Russ Tropp (John Russell) devises a scheme to recruit cheap labor to pick his cotton. He marries love-starved Cecile Steele (Lurene Tuttle), greases the right palms to get her elected judge, and has her send prisoners to his farm under the guise of a rehabilitation program. Tropp doesn't want any *real* criminals, so mostly what he's sent are teenagers, arrested for some petty crime, often on a trumped-up charge. The kids are housed in shacks with inadequate toilet facilities, sleep on canvas cots, and eat dog food disguised as beef stew. And the little money they earn is used for their clothing, food, and medical expenses. When confronted with these facts by her son, Judge Steele sobs that she can't help herself. But when she learns Tropp is fooling around with some of the young stuff on the farm she quickly sets things right again.

Most of the songs are performed by actress Mamie Van Doren, despite the presence of Eddie Cochran, who played the role of Bong. Born in Minnesota on October 3, 1938, Cochran was one of the many rockers heavily influenced by Elvis Presley. He'd already had a couple of hit records when he made this film. Why he was delegated a single number is anybody's guess.

Cochran taught himself to play the guitar when he was twelve, and by the time his family moved to Bell Gardens, California, in 1953 he was ready to rock and roll. He was playing at supermarket openings and local parties when he chanced to meet songwriter Jerry Capehart in a local record store. The two began writing songs for Cochran to sing, and

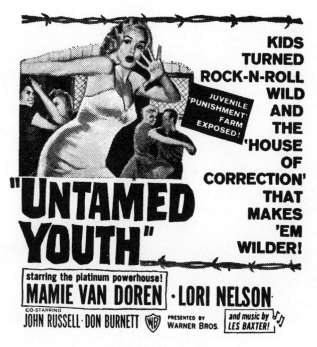

Ad for *Untamed Youth.*

before long Cochran had signed with Liberty Records. When 20th Century–Fox went looking for rockers to appear in their splashy comedy-rock musical *The Girl Can't Help It,* they drew heavily from the Liberty stable and Cochran was one of the performers selected. He sang "Twenty Flight Rock" which was supposed to be his first Liberty release in 1956. But Liberty wanted something that sounded more like Elvis and instead released "Sittin' in the Balcony," which became a hit.

"Eddie was blue-eyed and skinny, with curly blonde hair and an all–American smile that won me over right away," said Mamie Van Doren. In her autobiography, *Playing the Field,* Van Doren fondly recalled an afternoon at her house when her husband, Ray Anthony, was away at rehearsal and she and Cochran were doing a little rehearsing of their own. "All at once Eddie leaned over and kissed me. In a few moments we were in each other's arms. Suddenly the front door slammed—Ray was back from rehearsal! Eddie and I straightened ourselves out, and I flipped on the record player with one of [Eddie's] demos on it. A rock 'n' roll dance beat boomed out through the room." Anthony hated rock music so much he poked his head in just long

Mamie Van Doren rocks out in *Untamed Youth*.

enough to express his displeasure before storming off to his room. Had he not been in so much of a hurry he might have noticed their flushed faces.

Perhaps if *Untamed Youth* had been made the following year, Cochran would have had more to do in it. The year 1958 was his most successful period. In March of that year he and Capehart cowrote "Summertime Blues," Cochran's most successful record, now considered a rock classic. More hits followed as did television and concert appearances. He was supposed to tour with Buddy Holly and Ritchie Valens and would have been on the plane that killed them in 1959 had there not been a mix-up in his schedule. He told his friends he felt like he was living on borrowed time. The following year he was dead.

During a break in a five-month tour in England, Eddie Cochran, his girlfriend Sharon Shelley, Gene Vincent, and theatrical agent Patrick Thomkins were on their way to the airport when a tire blew. The car skidded backwards into a lamppost, and Cochran was flung from the car.

"When the three of us traveled together," said Vincent, "Shari always sat in the middle, but because of the crowd of fans, I got in the cab first, then Eddie, then Shari last. With Eddie in the middle, the only way he could have flown out that door was if he tried to cover Shari. The only way I came out alive was because I had taken a sleeping pill. After the crash, I woke up first and carried Eddie to the ambulance even though I had a broken arm. I was in such a state of shock that I thought nothing was wrong with me." Cochran died a little after four the following afternoon. His last record, released posthumously, was ironically titled "Three Steps to Heaven." He was one of the first 25 artists inducted in the Rock and Roll Hall of Fame.

Playing Mamie Van Doren's sister in *Untamed Youth* was former Universal-International contract player Lori Nelson (born Dixie Kay Nelson in Santa Fe, New Mexico, in 1933), who'd made her screen debut in one of the studio's Ma and Pa Kettle movies. She was on loan to RKO for almost a year, and by the time she returned in 1955 the studio regime had changed and her contract had been allowed to lapse. She appeared in several low-budgeters, and when she signed for *Untamed Youth* she'd been working with comedian-dancer Leon Tyler on a nightclub act. "The jitterbug number I did with him was not in the original script," said Nelson. "We did a little demonstration for Howard Koch, the director, and he put it in the movie."

A little guy with thick-rimmed glasses and a funny upturned hat, Leon Tyler can also be seen in *The Girl Can't Help It, Carnival Rock* and *Don't Knock the Rock* — in the latter dancing everyone off of the floor during Bill Haley's "Rip It Up" number.

The Music

Eddie Cochran: "Cotton Picker," available on Liberty.

Mamie Van Doren: "Go Go Calypso," "Oobala Baby," "Rollin' Stone," and "Salamander," originally released on a Prep EP with the first and last song also released as a single. The songs have recently resurfaced on Rhino Records on an LP with other songs by Mamie.

The Reception

"There are some good songs by Les Baxter and others and surprisingly good performances from Mamie Van Doren, Lori Nelson and a largely youthful cast. . . . The plot is not too important except for the

Lori Nelson and Eddie Cochran.

opportunity it gives for the musical numbers, both rock-and-roll and calypso, which are well integrated in the story and interestingly staged."—*The Hollywood Reporter.*

"Suited the teenage crowd as it has some rock 'n' roll numbers which are the fad at present."—Wayne Goodwin, an Indiana exhibitor.

"Best part of the picture is the driving beat of the music, four r&r pieces and one calypso, and it does more to hold the footage together than the actual story development."—*Variety.*

"The teenagers and a few adults came to see this and pronounced it 'right down their alley.'" — M.L. DuBose, a Texas exhibitor.

". . . is really fun, with its melodramatic combination of rock 'n' roll plus sex. That is, if you like rock 'n' roll. I do." — Ruth Waterbury.

"Good rock and roll picture. Played top time three days. Business good. Teenagers will see it two or more times." — Charlie C. Webb, Alabama exhibitor.

The Cast

Mamie Van Doren (Penny Low), Lori Nelson (Janey Low), John Russell (Russ Tropp), Don Burnett (Bob Steele), Eddie Cochran (Bong), Lurene Tuttle (Cecile Steele), Yvonne Lime (Baby), Jeanne Carmen (Lillibet), Robert Foulk (Mitch Bowers), Wayne Taylor (Duke), Jerry Barclay (Ralph), Keith Richards (Angelo), Valerie Reynolds (Arkie), Lucita (Margarita), Glenn Dixon (Landis), Wally Brown (Pinky), Michael Emmett (doctor).

The Credits

Director Howard W. Koch, *Producer* Aubrey Schenck, *Screenplay* John C. Higgens from a story by Stephen Longstreet, *Director of Photography* Carl Guthrie, *Assistant Director* Art Loel, *Editor* John F. Schreyer, *Sound* Robert Lee, *Music* Les Baxter. B&W 80 min. A Bel-Air Production. Released by Warner Bros.

Sources

Boxoffice, Vol. 71, No. 8, June 15, 1957, pg. 12; Vol. 71, No. 14, July 27, 1957, pg. 12; Vol. 71, No. 25, October 19, 1957, pg. 12; Herman, *Rock 'N' Roll Babylon;* Katz, *Film Encyclopedia;* Stambler, *Encyclopedia of Pop Rock and Soul;* Van Doren, *Playing the Field.*

Appendix A
Song–Film Reference List

Song Title	Film
"A.B.C. Boogie" (Russel, Spickel)	*Rock Around the Clock*
"Ain't That a Shame" (Domino, Bartholomew)	*Shake, Rattle and Rock!*
"All Love Broke Loose" (Singleton, Cathy)	*Let's Rock!*
"All Night Long"	*Carnival Rock*
"Angel Face"	*Go, Johnny, Go!*
"Annie Laurie" (Douglas, Scott)	*Hot Rod Gang*
"AppleJack" (D. Appell, E. Appell)	*Don't Knock the Rock!*
"As I Love You"	*The Big Beat*
"As Long as I Have You" (Wise, Weisman)	*King Creole*
"At the Hop" (Medora, White)	*Let's Rock!*
"Ave Maria" (Schubert)	*Girls Town*
"Baby Baby"	*Rock, Rock, Rock*
"Baby Blue"	*Hot Rod Gang*
"Baby I Don't Care" (Leiber, Stoller)	*Jailhouse Rock*
"Baby Wants to Rock"	*Rock, Rock, Rock*
"Barcelona Rock"	*Mister Rock and Roll*
"Be Bop a Lula" (Vincent, Davis)	*The Girl Can't Help It*
"Because They're Young" (Costa, Schroeder)	*Because They're Young*
"Believe Me"	*Hot Rod Gang*
"Beulah's Boogie"	*Rock 'n' Roll Revue*
"Big Band Rock 'N' Roll" (Mancini)	*Rock Pretty Baby*
"The Big Beat" (Domino, Bartholomew)	*The Big Beat*
"The Big Beat"	*Rock, Rock, Rock*
"Blast Off" (Jones)	*Let's Rock!*

177

"Blue Monday" (Domino, Bartholo-
mew)   *The Girl Can't Help It*

"Bop It"   *Rock Baby Rock It*
"A Broken Promise"   *Jamboree*
"Build Up"   *Rock Around the World*
"Bundle of Dreams"   *Sing Boy Sing*
"Butterfingers"   *Rock Around the World*
"Call Me"   *The Big Beat*
"Calling All Comets" (Haley,   *Don't Knock the Rock!*
Gabler, Pompilli)
"Calypso Boogie" (L. Baxter, J.   *Bop Girl Goes Calypso*
Baxter)
"Can I Steal a Little Love"   *Rock Pretty Baby!*
(Tuminello)
"Cannibal Pot"   *Rock Around the World*
"Casual" (Hackady, Gohman)   *Let's Rock!*
"Chicken in the Rough"   *Rock Baby Rock It*
"China Star"   *Rock Baby Rock It*
"Cinnamon Sinner"   *The Girl Can't Help It*
"Codfish and Potatoes"   *Rock Around the Clock*
"College Confidential"   *College Confidential*
"College Confidential Ball" (Twitty)   *College Confidential*
"Confess It to Your Heart"   *Mister Rock and Roll*
"Cool Baby"   *Jamboree*
"Cool It Baby"   *The Girl Can't Help It*
"Cotton Picker" (Baxter)   *Untamed Youth*
"Country Dance" (Jones)   *Don't Knock the Rock!*
"Crawfish" (Wise, Weisman)   *King Creole*
"Crazy 'Cause I Love You"   *Sing Boy Sing*
"Crazy Crazy Love"   *Rock Baby Rock It*
"Crazy Crazy Party" (Stone, Winley)   *Let's Rock!*
"Crazy to Care"   *Jamboree*
"The Creep"   *Carnival Rock*
"Cross Over"   *Jamboree*
"Cry Me a River" (Hamilton)   *The Girl Can't Help It*
"Cuero"   *Rock Around the Clock*
"Dance in the Street"   *Hot Rod Gang*
"Dancin' to the Bop"   *Hot Rod Gang*
"Dark Blue" (Mancini)   *Rock Pretty Baby!*
"De Rain" (Baxter, Adelson)   *Bop Girl Goes Calypso*
"Dixieland Rock" (Schroeder, Frank)   *King Creole*
"Don't Ask Me Why" (Wise,   *King Creole*
Weisman)
"Don't Be Afraid to Love"   *Go, Johnny, Go!*
"Don't Knock the Rock" (Karger,   *Don't Knock the Rock!*
Kent)
"Don't Leave Me Now" (Schroeder,   *Jailhouse Rock*
Weisman)

"Doomsday Rock"	*Rock Around the World*
"Drum Hi!"	*Mister Rock and Roll*
"Eat Your Heart Out"	*Rock Baby Rock It*
"Elevator Rock"	*Rock Around the World*
"Ever Since I Can Remember"	*Rock, Rock, Rock*
"Feelin' Happy"	*Shake, Rattle and Rock!*
"15 Cents"	*Rock Around the World*
"Fools Rush In" (Mercer, Bloom)	*Bop Girl Goes Calypso*
"For Children of All Ages"	*Jamboree*
"Fortunate Fella"	*Mr. Rock and Roll*
"Free and Easy" (Mancini)	*Rock Pretty Baby!*
"The Freeze"	*Juke Box Rhythm*
"Freight Train"	*Rock Around the World*
"Get Acquainted Waltz"	*Mister Rock and Roll*
"Get Out of the Car"	*Juke Box Rhythm*
"Girls Town" (Anka)	*Girls Town*
"Glad All Over"	*Jamboree*
"Go Go Calypso" (Baxter)	*Untamed Youth*
"Gone" (Rogers)	*Jamboree*
"Gonna Run" (D'Attili, De Jesus)	*Don't Knock the Rock!*
"Goofin' Around" (Beecher, Grande)	*Don't Knock the Rock!*
"Got a Lot o' Livin' to Do" (Schroeder, Weisman)	*Loving You*
"Great Balls of Fire" (Hammer, Blackwell)	*Jamboree*
"The Great Pretender" (Ram)	*Rock All Night* and *Rock Around the Clock*
"A Handful of Songs"	*Rock Around the World*
"Happy Baby"	*Rock Around the Clock*
"Hard Headed Woman" (DeMetrius)	*King Creole*
"Hard Rock and Candy Baby" (Baxter, Adelson)	*Bop Girl Goes Calypso*
"Heavenly Father"	*Go, Johnny, Go!*
"Hello Folks"	*Mister Rock and Roll*
"Here Comes Love" (Stone)	*Let's Rock!*
"He's Mine" (Taylor, Robi, Miles)	*Rock All Night*
"Hey, Juanita"	*Rock Baby Rock It*
"Hey, Mama" (Anka)	*Girls Town*
"Hey Poppa Rock"	*Mister Rock and Roll*
"High School Confidential" (Lewis, Hargrove)	*High School Confidential*
"Hit and Run Lover"	*Hot Rod Gang*
"Honey Chile"	*Shake, Rattle and Rock!*
"Hook, Line and Sinker" (Haley, Khoury, Bonner)	*Don't Knock the Rock!*
"Hot Dog" (Leiber, Stoller)	*Loving You*
"Hot Dog, Buddy, Buddy" (Haley)	*Don't Knock the Rock!*
"Hot Rock"	*Rock Baby Rock It*

"Hot Rod" (Mancini) — *Rock Pretty Baby!*

"Hula Love" (Knox) — *Jamboree*

"I Ain't Gonna Cry No More" — *The Girl Can't Help It*

"I Cry More" (David, Bacharach) — *Don't Knock the Rock!*

"I Don't Like You No More" — *Jamboree*

"I Feel It Right Here" — *Juke Box Rhythm*

"I Guess I Won't Hang Around Here Anymore" (Ram) — *Rock All Night*

"I Knew from the Start" (Moore, Subotsky) — *Rock, Rock, Rock*

"I Like Take Me Back, Baby" — *Rock Around the World*

"I Love You" (Anka) — *Girls Town*

"I Waited So Long" — *The Big Beat*

"I Wanna Rock Now" — *Rock All Night*

"I Want to Be Free" (Leiber, Stoller) — *Jailhouse Rock*

"I Was the Last One to Know" — *Mister Rock and Roll*

"If Not for You" — *Jamboree*

"I'll Be Waiting There for You" (Anka) — *Let's Rock!*

"I'll Stop Anything I'm Doing" — *Mister Rock and Roll*

"I'm Gonna Rock and Roll Till I Die" (Towne, Morris) — *Bop Girl Goes Calypso*

"I'm Gonna Walk and Talk with My Lord" — *Sing Boy, Sing*

"I'm in Love Again" — *Shake, Rattle and Rock!*

"I'm Not a Juvenile Delinquent" — *Rock, Rock, Rock*

"I'm Sorry" (Tinturin, White) — *Rock All Night*

"I'm Walking" (Domino, Bartholomew) — *The Big Beat*

"It Takes a Long, Long Time" — *Go, Johnny, Go!*

"It's Great When You're Doing a Show" — *The Big Beat*

"It's Simply Heavenly" — *Mister Rock and Roll*

"Jailhouse Rock" (Leiber, Stoller) — *Jailhouse Rock*

"Jamboree" — *Jamboree*

"Juke Box Rock" (Mancini) — *Rock Pretty Baby!*

"Just a Little Bit More" — *Sing Boy, Sing*

"Kiddio" — *Mister Rock and Roll*

"King Creole" (Leiber, Stoller) — *King Creole*

"Kool Kid" (Mancini) — *Rock Pretty Baby!*

"Last Night" — *Juke Box Rhythm*

"Lazy Love" — *The Big Beat*

"Let Me" (Presley, Matson) — *Love Me Tender*

"Let's Fall in Love" — *Juke Box Rhythm*

"Lipstick, Powder and Paint" — *Shake, Rattle and Rock!*

"Little Blue Wren" — *Rock, Rock, Rock*

"Little Darlin'" (Williams) — *The Big Beat*

"Little Queenie" (Berry) — *Go, Johnny, Go!*
"Lonely Boy" (Anka) — *Girls Town*
"Lonelyville" (Hackady, Marks) — *Let's Rock!*
"Lonesome" — *Rock Baby Rock It*
"Lonesome Cowboy" (Tepper, Bennett) — *Loving You*
"Lonesome Train" — *Rock, Rock, Rock*
"Long Tall Sally" (Johnson) — *Don't Knock the Rock!*
"Love Me Baby" — *Rock Baby Rock It*
"Love Me Right (in the Morning)" — *Mister Rock and Roll*
"Love Me Tender" (Presley, Matson, Poulton) — *Love Me Tender*
"Love Never Forgets" — *Rock Baby Rock It*
"Lover Doll" (Wayne) — *King Creole*
"Loving You" (Leiber, Stoller) — *Loving You*
"Make Me Love Again" — *Mr. Rock and Roll*
"Make Room for Joy" — *Juke Box Rhythm*
"Mama, Can I Go Out" — *Go Johnny, Go!*
"Mambo Capri" — *Rock Around the Clock*
"Mambo Rock" — *Rock Around the Clock*
"Mean Woman Blues" (De Metrius) — *Loving You*
"Memphis, Tennessee" (Berry) — *Go Johnny, Go!*
"Midnight Sun" — *Rock 'n' Roll Revue*
"Mister Rock and Roll" — *Mister Rock and Roll*
"The Mooch" — *Rock 'n' Roll Revue*
"The Most" (Mancini) — *Rock Pretty Baby*
"The Mushroom Song" (Sullivan) — *Giant Gila Monster*
"My Baby She Rocks" (Sullivan) — *Giant Gila Monster*
"My Idea of Love" — *The Girl Can't Help It*
"My Love Is Strong" — *Go Johnny, Go!*
"New Orleans" (Tepper, Bennett) — *King Creole*
"Now the Day Is Over" — *Go Johnny, Go!*
"Oh Baby Doll" (Berry) — *Mister Rock and Roll*
"Oh! My Head" (Valens) — *Go Johnny, Go!*
"Oke-she-moke-she-pop" — *Rock 'n' Roll Revue*
"Once Again" — *Go Johnny, Go!*
"One and Only" — *Carnival Rock*
"One O'Clock Jump" — *Jamboree*
"Only a Moment Ago" — *Rock 'n' Roll Revue*
"Oo Ba Lo" (Baxter, Adelson) — *Bop Girl Goes Calypso*
"Oobala Baby" (Baxter, Adelson, Cockran, Capehart) — *Untamed Youth*
"Ou-Shoo-Bla-D" — *Carnival Rock*
"Out of the Bushes" (Moore, Mills) — *Don't Knock the Rock!*
"Over and Over Again" (B. Weisman, A. Weisman) — *Rock, Rock, Rock*
"Party" (Robinson) — *Loving You*
"Pathway to Sin" — *Mister Rock and Roll*

"People in Love"   *Sing Boy, Sing*
"Perfect for Love"   *Mister Rock and Roll*
"Picnic by the Sea" (Troup,   *Rock Pretty Baby!*
  McKuen)
"Playmates"   *College Confidential*
"Playmates"   *Go Johnny, Go!*
"Poor Boy" (Presley, Matson)   *Love Me Tender*
"Puppy Love"   *Blood of Dracula*
"Razzle Dazzle" (Calhoun)   *Rock Around the Clock*
"Record Hop Tonight"   *Jamboree*
"Rhythm in Blues" (Carter)   *Bop Girl Goes Calypso*
"Right Now"   *Rock, Rock, Rock*
"Rip It Up" (Blackwell, Marascalo)   *Don't Knock the Rock!*
"R-O-C-K"   *Rock Around the Clock*
"Rock-a-Beatin' Boogie" (Haley)   *Rock Around the Clock*
"Rock-A-Boogie"   *Carnival Rock*
"Rock All Night" (Ram)   *Rock All Night*
"Rock and Cry"   *Mister Rock and Roll*
"Rock and Roll Guitar" (Ram)   *Rock All Night*
"Rock Around the Clock" (Freed-   *Rock Around the Clock*
  man, De Knight)
"Rock Around the Rock Pile"   *Girl Can't Help It*
"Rock Baby Rock It"   *Rock Baby Rock It*
"Rock of Ages"   *Sing Boy, Sing*
"Rock Pretty Baby" (Burke)   *Rock Pretty Baby!*
"Rock, Rock, Rock"   *Rock, Rock, Rock*
"Rockabye Lullabye Blues" (Troup)   *Rock Pretty Baby!*
"Rockin' Is Our Business"   *The Girl Can't Help It*
"Rockin' Matbelle"   *Rock Baby Rock It*
"Rockin' on Saturday Night"   *Shake, Rattle and Rock!*
"Rockin' on Sunday Night" (Holtz-   *Don't Knock the Rock!*
  man, Ellis)
"Rockin' the Boogie" (Mancini)   *Rock Pretty Baby!*
"Rollin' Stone" (Baxter, Adelson)   *Untamed Youth*
"Roogie Doogie"   *Rock Baby Rock It*
"Rovin' Gal" (L. Baxter, J. Baxter)   *Bop Girl Goes Calypso*
"Rudy's Rock"   *Rock Around the Clock*
"Rumble on the Docks" (Phillips,   *Rumble on the Docks*
  De Knight)
"Sad and Lonely"   *Rock Around the Clock*
"The Saints Come Rockin' In"   *Rock Baby Rock It*
"Salamander" (Baxter)   *Untamed Youth*
"See You Later, Alligator" (Guidry)   *Rock Around the Clock*
"Shazam" (Eddy, Hazelwood)   *Because They're Young*
"Ship on a Stormy Sea"   *Go Johnny, Go!*
"Short Shorts" (Austin, Gaudio)   *Let's Rock!*
"Siempre"   *Jamboree*
"Sing Boy, Sing" (Sands, McKuen)   *Sing Boy Sing*

"So Be It" (Allen)   *College Confidential*
"So Hard to Laugh, So Easy to Cry"   *Bop Girl Goes Calypso*
  (Askam, Carter)
"Soda Pop Pop"   *Sing Boy Sing*
"Special Date" (Cavanaugh, Smalley)   *Frankenstein's Daughter*
"Spread the Word"   *The Girl Can't Help It*
"Spring Is the Time for Remember-   *Juke Box Rhythm*
  ing"
"Star Rocket"   *Mister Rock and Roll*
"Steadfast, Loyal and True" (Leiber,   *King Creole*
  Stoller)
"Sweet Love on My Mind"   *Shake, Rattle and Rock!*
"Swingin' School" (Mann, Lowe)   *Because They're Young*
"Take My Heart"   *The Big Beat*
"Take the First Train Out of Town"   *Rumble on the Docks*
  (B. Latanzi, P. Latanzi)
"Take the 'T' Train"   *Rock 'n' Roll Revue*
"Teacher's Pet"   *Jamboree*
"Tears Keep Tumbling Down"   *Rock 'n' Roll Revue*
"Teddy Bear" (Mann, Lowe)   *Loving You*
"Teen Age Bop" (Mancini)   *Rock Pretty Baby!*
"Teen Age Frankie and Johnnie"   *Carnival Rock*
"Teenage Party"   *Rock Around the World*
"Tempo's Tempo" (Tempo)   *The Girl Can't Help It*
"Thanks to You"   *Rock, Rock, Rock*
"That's All I Want from You"   *Sing Boy Sing*
"That's Never Happened to Me"   *Rock, Rock, Rock*
"There Are Times" (Hackady,   *Let's Rock!*
  Gohman)
"There's No Place Without You"   *Carnival Rock*
"This Is the Night"   *Carnival Rock*
"This Moment of Love"   *Mister Rock and Roll*
"Time to Cry" (Anka)   *Girls Town*
"Time to Kill"   *Rock Around the World*
"Toreador"   *Jamboree*
"Tra-La-La"   *Rock, Rock, Rock*
"Treat Me Nice" (Leiber, Stoller)   *Jailhouse Rock*
"Trouble" (Leiber, Stoller)   *King Creole*
"The Trouble with You Is Me"   *Rock 'n' Roll Revue*
"Tutti Frutti" (Penniman, La   *Don't Knock the Rock!*
  Bostrie, Lubin)
"20 Flight Rock" (Fairchild,   *The Girl Can't Help It*
  Cochran)
"Twenty-Four Hours a Day"   *Jamboree*
"Two Eyes"   *Rock Around the World*
"Two Perfect Strangers" (Hackady,   *Let's Rock!*
  Gohman)
"Vip-i-ty Vip-i-ty Vop"   *Rock 'n' Roll Revue*

"Wait and See" (Domino, Bartholomew)	*Jamboree*
"Water, Water"	*Rock Around the World*
"Way Back in San Francisco" (Baxter, Adelson)	*Bop Girl Goes Calypso*
"We're Gonna Move" (Presley, Matson)	*Love Me Tender*
"We're Gonna Rock Tonight"	*Rock, Rock, Rock*
"What More Do You Want Me to Do"	*Rock 'n' Roll Revue*
"What's It Gonna Be" (Carey, Mancini)	*Rock Pretty Baby!*
"Where Mary Go" (Lampert, Gluck)	*The Big Beat*
"Who Are We to Say"	*Jamboree*
"Who Baby"	*Sing Boy Sing*
"Wild Wild Women"	*Rock Baby Rock It*
"Will It Be You?"	*Rock Around the World*
"Willie and the Hand Jive"	*Juke Box Rhythm*
"Wish It Were Me" (Ram)	*Girls Town*
"Won't You Give Me a Chance?"	*Rock, Rock, Rock*
"Would I Be Crying?" (Moore)	*Rock, Rock, Rock*
"Would I Love You?"	*Sing Boy Sing*
"Wow" (Winley, Clowney, Kornegay)	*Bop Girl Goes Calypso*
"You Can't Catch Me" (Berry)	*Rock, Rock, Rock*
"You Done Me Wrong"	*Go, Johnny, Go!*
"You Gotta Go"	*Rock Around the World*
"You'd Better Know It" (Wilson, Henry)	*Go, Johnny, Go!*
"You'll Be There"	*Mister Rock and Roll*
"You'll Have the Things Your Heart Needs"	*Rock, Rock, Rock*
"You'll Never, Never Know" (Miles, Robi, Williams)	*The Girl Can't Help It*
"Young and Beautiful" (Silver, Schroeder)	*Jailhouse Rock*
"Young Dreams" (Kalmanoff)	*King Creole*
"Young Love" (Mancini)	*Rock Pretty Baby!*
"Your Cash Ain't Nothin' But Trash"	*Rock 'n' Roll Revue*
"Your Daddy Wants to Do Right"	*Sing Boy Sing*
"Your Love Is My Love" (Edwards)	*Don't Knock the Rock!*
"You're Being Followed"	*The Big Beat*
"You're So Right" (D'Attili, De Jesus)	*Don't Knock the Rock!*
"You've Got to Have Ee-ooo" (Dunlap, Redwine)	*How to Make a Monster*
"You've Never Been in Love"	*The Big Beat*

Appendix B
Performer–Song Reference List

Steve Allen
"So Be It"   *College Confidential*
Paul Anka
"Ave Maria"   *Girls Town*
"Girls Town"   *Girls Town*
"I'll Be Waiting There for You"   *Let's Rock!*
"Lonely Boy"   *Girls Town*
"A Time to Cry"   *Girls Town*
Ray Anthony
"Rock Around the Rock Pile"   *The Girl Can't Help It*
Dave Appell and His Applejacks
"Applejack"   *Don't Knock the Rock!*
"Country Dance"   *Don't Knock the Rock!*
"Don't Knock the Rock"   *Don't Knock the Rock!*
"Gonna Run"   *Don't Knock the Rock!*
"I Cry More"   *Don't Knock the Rock!*
"You're So Right"   *Don't Knock the Rock!*
John Ashley
"Annie Laurie"   *Hot Rod Gang*
"Believe Me"   *Hot Rod Gang*
"Hit and Run Lover"   *Hot Rod Gang*
"You've Got to Have Ee-ooo"   *How to Make a Monster*
Frankie Avalon
"Teacher's Pet"   *Jamboree*
La Vern Baker
"Humpty Dumpty Heart"   *Mister Rock and Roll*
"Love Me Right (in the Morning)"   *Mister Rock and Roll*
"Tra-La-La"   *Rock, Rock, Rock*
The Bellew Twins
"Lonesome"   *Rock Baby Rock It*
"Love Me Baby"   *Rock Baby Rock It*

185

Freddie Bell and His Bellboys

"Giddy Up Ding Dong"	*Rock Around the Clock*
"Rumble on the Docks"	*Rumble on the Docks*
"Take the First Train Out of Town"	*Rumble on the Docks*
"We're Gonna Teach You to Rock"	*Rock Around the Clock*

Jerry Blaine

"Puppy Love"	*Blood of Dracula*

Chuck Berry

"La Juanda"	*Mister Rock and Roll*
"Little Queenie"	*Go, Johnny, Go!*
"Memphis, Tennessee"	*Go, Johnny, Go!*
"Oh Baby Doll"	*Mister Rock and Roll*
"You Can't Catch Me"	*Rock, Rock, Rock*

The Blockbusters

"I Wanna Rock Now"	*Rock All Night*
"Ou-Shoo-Bla-D"	*Carnival Rock*
"Rock All Night"	*Rock All Night*
"Rock-A-Boogie"	*Carnival Rock*
"Rock and Roll Guitar"	*Rock All Night*
"There's No Place Without You"	*Carnival Rock*

Jimmy Bowen

"Cross Over"	*Jamboree*

Ruth Brown

"Tears Keep Tumbling Down"	*Rock 'n' Roll Revue*

Sonny Burke

"Rock Pretty Baby"	*Rock Pretty Baby!*

Johnny Burnette Trio

"The Big Red"	*Rock, Rock, Rock*
"Rock, Rock, Rock"	*Rock, Rock, Rock*

Susan Cabot

"Ou-Shoo-Bla-D"	*Carnival Rock*
"There's No Place Without You"	*Carnival Rock*

The Cadillacs

"Jay Walker"	*Go, Johnny, Go!*
"Please Mr. Johnson"	*Go, Johnny, Go!*

Jo Ann Campbell

"Mama, Can I Go Out"	*Go, Johnny, Go!*

Page Cavanaugh Trio

"Special Date"	*Frankenstein's Daughter*

Paul Carr

"If Not for You"	*Jamboree*
"Twenty-Four Hours a Day"	*Jamboree*
"Who Are We to Say?"	*Jamboree*

Johnny Carroll

"Crazy Crazy Love"	*Rock Baby Rock It*
"Rock Baby Rock It"	*Rock Baby Rock It*
"Rockin' Matbelle"	*Rock Baby Rock It*

"Wild Wild Women"   *Rock Baby Rock It*
Tommy Charles
"Sweet Love on My Mind"   *Shake, Rattle and Rock!*
The Chuckles
"Cinnamon Sinner"   *The Girl Can't Help It*
Cirno and the Bowties
"Ever Since I Can Remember"   *Rock, Rock, Rock*
Jimmy Clanton
"Angel Face"   *Go, Johnny, Go!*
"It Takes a Long, Long Time"   *Go, Johnny, Go!*
"My Love Is Strong"   *Go, Johnny, Go!*
"Now the Day Is Over"   *Go, Johnny, Go!*
"Once Again"   *Go, Johnny, Go!*
"Ship on a Stormy Sea"   *Go, Johnny, Go!*
"You Done Me Wrong"   *Go, Johnny, Go!*
The Clovers
"Your Cash Ain't Nothin' But   *Rock 'n' Roll Revue*
   Trash"
Don Coates and the Bon Aires
"China Star"   *Rock Baby Rock It*
"Love Never Forgets"   *Rock Baby Rock It*
Eddie Cochran
"Cotton Picker"   *Untamed Youth*
"Teenage Heaven"   *Go, Johnny, Go!*
"20 Flight Rock"   *The Girl Can't Help It*
Shaye Cogan
"Get Acquainted Waltz"   *Mister Rock and Roll*
"Pathway to Sin"   *Mister Rock and Roll*
Ron Colby
"Toreador"   *Jamboree*
Nat "King" Cole
"The Trouble with You Is Me"   *Rock 'n' Roll Revue*
Alan Copeland and Russ Morgan
"As I Love You"   *The Big Beat*
Count Basie
"Jamboree"   *Jamboree*
"One O'Clock Jump"   *Jamboree*
Kathy Crosby
"I Love You"   *Girls Town*
Alan Dale
"Don't Knock the Rock"   *Don't Knock the Rock!*
"Gonna Run"   *Don't Knock the Rock!*
"I Cry More"   *Don't Knock the Rock!*
"Your Love Is My Love"   *Don't Knock the Rock!*
"You're So Right"   *Don't Knock the Rock!*
Danny and the Juniors
"At the Hop"   *Let's Rock!*
Larry Darnell

"What Do You Want Me to Do?"	*Rock 'n' Roll Revue*
James Darren	
"Because They're Young"	*Because They're Young*
Martha Davis	
"Vip-i-ty, Vip-i-ty Vop"	*Rock 'n' Roll Revue*
Delta Rhythm Boys	
"Take the 'T' Train"	*Rock 'n' Roll Revue*
The Diamonds	
"Little Darlin'"	*The Big Beat*
"Where Mary Go"	*The Big Beat*
Fats Domino	
"Ain't That a Shame"	*Shake, Rattle and Rock!*
"Blue Monday"	*The Girl Can't Help It*
"Honey Chile"	*Shake, Rattle and Rock!*
"I'm in Love Again"	*Shake, Rattle and Rock!*
"Wait and See"	*Jamboree*
Duane Eddy	
"Shazam"	*Because They're Young*
Duke Ellington	
"The Mooch"	*Rock 'n' Roll Revue*
Five Stars	
"Hey Juanita"	*Rock Baby Rock It*
"Your Love Is All I Need"	*Rock Baby Rock It*
The Flamingos	
"Jump Children"	*Go, Johnny, Go!*
"Would I Be Crying?"	*Rock, Rock, Rock*
Eddie Fontaine	
"Cool It Baby"	*The Girl Can't Help It*
The Four Aces	
"Take My Heart"	*The Big Beat*
The Four Coins	
"A Broken Promise"	*Jamboree*
Connie Francis	
"For Children of All Ages"	*Jamboree*
"Little Blue Wren"	*Rock, Rock, Rock*
"Siempre"	*Jamboree*
"That's Never Happened to Me"	*Rock, Rock, Rock*
"Twenty-Four Hours a Day"	*Jamboree*
"Who Are We to Say?"	*Jamboree*
The Goofers	
"I'm Gonna Rock and Roll Till I Die"	*Bop Girl Goes Calypso*
Roscoe Gordon and the Red Tops	
"Bop It"	*Rock Baby Rock It*
"Chicken in the Rough"	*Rock Baby Rock It*
Charlie Gracie	
"Cool Baby"	*Jamboree*
Earl Grant Trio	

"I Feel It Right Here"   *Juke Box Rhythm*
"Last Night"   *Juke Box Rhythm*
Gogi Grant
"Call Me"   *The Big Beat*
"Lazy Love"   *The Big Beat*
"You've Never Been in   *The Big Beat*
  Love"
Bill Haley and His Comets
"A.B.C. Boogie"   *Rock Around the Clock*
"Calling All Comets"   *Don't Knock the Rock!*
"Don't Knock the Rock"   *Don't Knock the Rock!*
"Goofin' Around"   *Don't Knock the Rock!*
"Happy Baby"   *Rock Around the Clock*
"Hook, Line and Sinker"   *Don't Knock the Rock!*
"Hot Dog, Buddy, Buddy"   *Don't Knock the Rock!*
"Mambo Rock"   *Rock Around the Clock*
"Razzle Dazzle"   *Rock Around the Clock*
"Rip It Up"   *Don't Knock the Rock!*
"R-O-C-K"   *Rock Around the Clock*
"Rock Around the Clock"   *Rock Around the Clock*
"Rock-a-Beatin' Boogie"   *Rock Around the Clock*
"Rudy's Rock"   *Rock Around the Clock*
"See You Later, Alligator"   *Rock Around the Clock*
Roy Hamilton
"Here Comes Love"   *Let's Rock!*
Lionel Hampton
"Beulah's Boogie"   *Rock 'n' Roll Revue*
"Drum Hi!"   *Mister Rock and Roll*
"Hello Folks"   *Mister Rock and Roll*
"Hey Poppa Rock"   *Mister Rock and Roll*
"Midnight Sun"   *Rock 'n' Roll Revue*
"Mister Rock and Roll"   *Mister Rock and Roll*
"Star Rocket"   *Mister Rock and Roll*
Martha Lou Harp
"Crazy to Care"   *Jamboree*
Harvey
"Don't Be Afraid to Love"   *Go, Johnny, Go!*
Nora Hayes
"The Great Pretender"   *Rock All Night*
"I Guess I Won't Hang Around   *Rock All Night*
  Here Anymore"
David Houston
"One and Only"   *Carnival Rock*
"Teen Age Frankie and Johnnie" *Carnival Rock*
Ferlin Husky
"Make Me Love Again"   *Mister Rock and Roll*
"This Moment of Love"   *Mister Rock and Roll*
George Jessel

"Spring Is the Time for Remembering"	*Juke Box Rhythm*
Jack Jones	
"The Freeze"	*Juke Box Rhythm*
"Make Room for Joy"	*Juke Box Rhythm*
Buddy Knox	
"Hula Love"	*Jamboree*
Julius La Rosa	
"Casual"	*Let's Rock!*
"Crazy, Crazy Party"	*Let's Rock!*
"There Are Times"	*Let's Rock!*
"Two Perfect Strangers"	*Let's Rock!*
Jerry Lee Lewis	
"Great Balls of Fire"	*Jamboree*
"High School Confidential"	*Jamboree*
Abbey Lincoln	
"Spread the Word"	*The Girl Can't Help It*
Little Richard	
"The Girl Can't Help It"	*The Girl Can't Help It*
"Long Tall Sally"	*Don't Knock the Rock!*
"Lucille"	*Mister Rock and Roll*
"Rip It Up"	*The Girl Can't Help It*
"She's Got It"	*The Girl Can't Help It*
"Tutti Frutti"	*Don't Knock the Rock!*
Julie London	
"Cry Me a River"	*The Girl Can't Help It*
Lord Flea	
"Calypso Jamboree"	*Bop Girl Goes Calypso*
Bob Luman and the Shadows	
"All Night Long"	*Carnival Rock*
"The Creep"	*Carnival Rock*
"This Is the Night"	*Carnival Rock*
Frankie Lyman and the Teenagers	
"Baby Baby"	*Rock, Rock, Rock*
"Fortunate Fella"	*Mister Rock and Roll*
"I'm Not a Juvenile Delinquent"	*Rock, Rock, Rock*
"Love Put Me Out of My Head"	*Mister Rock and Roll*
Lewis Lymon and the Teenchords	
"Gone"	*Jamboree*
Henry Mancini	
"Big Band Rock 'N' Roll"	*Rock Pretty Baby*
"Dark Blue"	*Rock Pretty Baby*
"Free and Easy"	*Rock Pretty Baby*
"Hot Rod"	*Rock Pretty Baby*
"Juke Box Rock"	*Rock Pretty Baby*
"Kool Kid"	*Rock Pretty Baby*
"The Most"	*Rock Pretty Baby*
"Rockin' the Boogie"	*Rock Pretty Baby*

"Teen Age Bop"   *Rock Pretty Baby*
"What's It Gonna Be?"   *Rock Pretty Baby*
"Young Love"   *Rock Pretty Baby*
Andy Martin
"Record Hop Tonight"   *Jamboree*
Wink Martindale
"All Love Broke Loose"   *Let's Rock!*
Rod McKuen
"Happy Is a Boy Named Me"   *Rock Pretty Baby*
"Picnic by the Sea"   *Rock Pretty Baby*
Clyde McPhatter
"Rock and Cry"   *Mister Rock and Roll*
"You'll Be There"   *Mister Rock and Roll*
The Mills Brothers
"You're Being Followed"   *The Big Beat*
The Moonglows
"Barcelona Rock"   *Mister Rock and Roll*
"Confess It to Your Heart"   *Mister Rock and Roll*
"I Knew from the Start"   *Rock, Rock, Rock*
"Over and Over Again"   *Rock, Rock, Rock*
Jo Morrow
"Let's Fall in Love"   *Juke Box Rhythm*
Lois O'Brien
"It's Simply Heavenly"   *Mister Rock and Roll*
Johnny Oleen
"I Ain't Gonna Cry No More"   *The Girl Can't Help It*
"My Idea of Love"   *The Girl Can't Help It*
Johnny Otis
"Willie and the Hand Jive"   *Juke Box Rhythm*
The Paulette Sisters, Rose Marie,
The Lancers
"It's Great When You're Doing a   *The Big Beat*
  Show"
Carl Perkins
"Glad All Over"   *Jamboree*
The Platters
"The Great Pretender"   *Rock Around the Clock*
"He's Mine"   *Rock All Night*
"I Love You"   *Girls Town*
"I'm Sorry"   *Rock All Night*
"Remember When"   *Carnival Rock*
"Wish It Were Me"   *Girls Town*
"You'll Never, Never Know"   *The Girl Can't Help It*
Preacher Smith and the Deacons
"Eat Your Heart Out"   *Rock Baby Rock It*
"Roogie Doogie"   *Rock Baby Rock It*
Elvis Presley
"As Long as I Have You"   *King Creole*

"(You're So Square) Baby I Don't Care" — *Jailhouse Rock*
"Crawfish" — *King Creole*
"Dixieland Rock" — *King Creole*
"Don't Ask Me Why" — *King Creole*
"Don't Leave Me Now" — *Jailhouse Rock*
"Got a Lot o' Livin' to Do" — *Loving You*
"Hard Headed Woman" — *King Creole*
"Hot Dog" — *Loving You*
"I Want to Be Free" — *Jailhouse Rock*
"Jailhouse Rock" — *Jailhouse Rock*
"King Creole" — *King Creole*
"Let Me" — *Love Me Tender*
"Lonesome Cowboy" — *Loving You*
"Love Me Tender" — *Love Me Tender*
"Lover Doll" — *King Creole*
"Loving You" — *Loving You*
"Mean Woman Blues" — *Loving You*
"New Orleans" — *King Crole*
"Party" — *Loving You*
"Poor Boy" — *Love Me Tender*
"Steadfast, Loyal and True" — *King Creole*
"Treat Me Nice" — *Jailhouse Rock*
"Trouble" — *King Creole*
"We're Gonna Move" — *Love Me Tender*
"Young and Beautiful" — *Jailhouse Rock*
"Young Dreams" — *King Creole*

Teddy Randazzo
"I'll Stop Anything I'm Doing" — *Mister Rock and Roll*
"I Was the Last One to Know" — *Mister Rock and Roll*
"Kiddio" — *Mister Rock and Roll*
"Perfect for Love" — *Mister Rock and Roll*
"Thanks to You" — *Rock, Rock, Rock*
"We're Gonna Rock Tonight" — *Rock, Rock, Rock*
"You Won't Give Me a Chance" — *Rock, Rock, Rock*
"You'll Have the Things Your Heart Needs" — *Rock, Rock, Rock*

Anita Ray
"Rockin' on Saturday Night" — *Shake, Rattle and Rock!*

Della Reese
"Lonelyville" — *Let's Rock!*

The Royal Teens
"Short Shorts" — *Let's Rock!*

Bobby Rydell
"Swingin' School" — *Because They're Young*

Tommy Sands
"Bundle of Dreams" — *Sing Boy Sing*
"Crazy 'Cause I Love You" — *Sing Boy Sing*

"I'm Gonna Walk and Talk with   *Sing Boy Sing*
  My Lord"
"Just a Little Bit More"   *Sing Boy Sing*
"People in Love"   *Sing Boy Sing*
"Rock of Ages"   *Sing Boy Sing*
"Sing Boy, Sing"   *Sing Boy Sing*
"Soda Pop Pop"   *Sing Boy Sing*
"That's All I Want from You"   *Sing Boy Sing*
"Who Baby"   *Sing Boy Sing*
"Would I Love You"   *Sing Boy Sing*
"Your Daddy Wants to Do Right"   *Sing Boy Sing*
Ivy Schulman
"Baby Wants to Rock"   *Rock, Rock, Rock*
Al Sears
"Thanks to You"   *Rock, Rock, Rock*
George Shearing Quintet
"As I Love You"   *The Big Beat*
Jeri Southern
"I Waited So Long"   *The Big Beat*
Randy Sparks
"College Confidential"   *College Confidential*
Sandy Stewart
"Heavenly Father"   *Go, Johnny, Go!*
"Playmates"   *Go, Johnny, Go!*
Don Sullivan
"The Mushroom Song"   *Giant Gila Monster*
"My Baby She Rocks"   *Giant Gila Monster*
Nino Tempo
"Horn Rock"   *Bop Girl Goes Calypso*
"Tempo's Tempo"   *The Girl Can't Help It*
Cal Tjader Quintet
"I Waited So Long"   *The Big Beat*
The Treniers
"Get Out of the Car"   *Juke Box Rhythm*
"Out of the Bushes"   *Don't Knock the Rock!*
"Rockin' Is Our Business"   *The Girl Can't Help It*
"Rockin' on Sunday Night"   *Don't Knock the Rock!*
Bobby Troup
"Rockabye Lullabye Blues"   *Rock Pretty Baby*
"Picnic by the Sea"   *Rock Pretty Baby*
Phil Tuminello
"Can I Steal a Little Love"   *Rock Pretty Baby*
Joe Turner
"Feelin' Happy"   *Shake, Rattle and Rock!*
"Lipstick, Powder and Paint"   *Shake, Rattle and Rock!*
"Oke-she-moke-she-pop"   *Rock 'n' Roll Revue*
Conway Twitty
"College Confidential Ball"   *College Confidential*

The Tyrones
"Blast Off"   *Let's Rock!*
Ritchie Valens
"Oh! My Head!"   *Go, Johnny, Go!*
Mamie Van Doren
"Go Go Calypso"   *Untamed Youth*
"Hey, Mama"   *Girls Town*
"Oobala Baby"   *Untamed Youth*
"Rollin' Stone"   *Untamed Youth*
"Salamander"   *Untamed Youth*
Gene Vincent
"Baby Blue"   *Hot Rod Gang*
"Be Bop a Lula"   *The Girl Can't Help It*
"Dance in the Street"   *Hot Rod Gang*
"Dancin' to the Bop"   *Hot Rod Gang*
Dinah Washington
"Only a Moment Ago"   *Rock 'n' Roll Revue*
Slim Whitman
"Unchain My Heart"   *Jamboree*
Joe Williams
"I Don't Like You No More"   *Jamboree*
Jackie Wilson
"You'd Better Know It"   *Go, Johnny, Go!*

Bibliography

Berry, Chuck. *Chuck Berry, the Autobiography.* New York: Harmony, 1987.
Boxoffice magazine, Vol. 70, No. 1 (Oct. 27, 1956)–Vol. 75, No. 26 (Oct. 19, 1959).
Bronson, Fred. *The Billboard Book of Number One Hits.* New York: Billboard Publications, 1988.
Brooks, Tim, and Earle Marsh. *The Complete Directory to Prime Time Network TV Shows.* New York: Ballantine, 1979.
Carr, Roy, and Mick Farren. *Elvis, the Illustrated Record.* New York: Harmony, 1982.
Clark, Alan. *Rock and Roll in the Movies.* No. 1. National Rock and Roll Archives.
Dowdy, Andrew. *The Films of the Fifties.* New York: Morrow, 1973.
Escott, Colin. "Jerry Lee Lewis, the Ferriday Wild Man." *Goldmine* 15 no. 14 (July 14, 1989): 7–9.
Herman, Gary. *Rock 'n' Roll Babylon.* Pennsylvania: Courage, 1987.
Hillman, Robert. "Farewell to Bill Haley, Rock's First Big Star." *Calendar* (February 15, 1981): 71.
Jenkinson, Philip, and Alan Warner. *Celluloid Rock.* London: Lorimer, 1974.
Katz, Ephraim. *The Film Encyclopedia.* New York: Putnam, 1979.
Lamparski, Richard. *Whatever Became of. . .?* Vol. 10. New York: Harmony, 1987.
Larson, Randall D. "The Film Music of Ronald Stein." *Cinemascore* (1984–85): 26.
Lichter, Paul. *Elvis in Hollywood.* New York: Simon & Schuster, 1975.
Luijters, Guus, and Gerard Timmer. *The Life and Death of Jayne Mansfield.* Secaucus, N.J.: Citadel, 1987.
McCarthy, Todd, and Charles Flynn. *Kings of the Bs.* New York: Dutton, 1975.
McCarty, John, and Mark Thomas McGee. *The Little Shop of Horrors Book.* New York: St. Martin's, 1988.
"Mike Connelly's Exclusive Report from Hollywood." *Screen Stories* (May 1957): 5.
Miller, Jim. *The Rolling Stone Illustrated History of Rock & Roll.* New York: Random House, 1980.

Naha, Ed. *The Films of Roger Corman: Brilliance on a Budget.* New York: Arco, 1982.

Nite, Norm N. *Rock On: The Illustrated Encyclopedia of Rock 'n' Roll.* New York: Harper & Row, 1982.

Pareles, Jon, and Patricia Romanowski. *The Rolling Stone Encyclopedia of Rock & Roll.* New York: Rolling Stone/Summit, 1983.

Peary, Danny. *Cult Movies.* New York: Dell, 1986.

Ragan, David. *Who's Who in Hollywood.* New York: Arlington House, 1976.

Stambler, Irwin. *The Encyclopedia of Pop Rock and Soul.* New York: St. Martin's, 1989.

Terrace, Vincent. *Complete Encyclopedia of Television Programs 1947–1979.* New York: Barnes, 1979.

Uslan, Michael, and Bruce Solomon. *Dick Clark's The First 25 Years of Rock and Roll.* New York: Greenwich House, 1981.

Van Doren, Mamie, with Art Aveilhe. *Playing the Field.* New York: Putnam, 1988.

Warren, Bill. *Keep Watching the Skies! American Science Fiction Movies of the Fifties.* Vol. II: 1958–1962. Jefferson, N.C., and London: McFarland, 1986.

White, Charles. *The Life and Times of Little Richard, the Quasar of Rock.* New York: Harmony, 1987.

White, Timothy. *Rock Stars.* New York: Stewart, Tabori and Chang, 1984.

Index